Contents

Outline of Numbers and Deuteronomy

Numbers

I. The Israelites Prepare to Depart (1:1–10:10)
   A. Moses takes a census (1:1-54)
   B. The position of the camps (2:1-34)
   C. The duties of the Levites (3:1-51)
   D. Census of the Levites (4:1-49)
   E. Laws and instructions (5:1–6:21)
   F. Aaron's Blessing on the People (6:22-27)
   G. Consecration of the tabernacle (7:1-89)
   H. Consecration of the Levites (8:1-26)
   J. Miscellaneous laws (9:1–10:10)

II. The Israelites Journey to Kadesh (10:11–21:13)
   A. The tribes leave Sinai (10:11-36)
   B. The Israelites murmur in the wilderness (11:1-35)
   C. Miriam is punished (12:1-16)
   D. The Israelites spy on Canaan (13:1-33)
   E. The Israelites attack Canaan (14:1-45)
   F. Laws concerning offerings (15:1-41)
   G. Korah rebels against Moses (16:1-50)
   H. Aaron's rod blossoms (17:1-13)
   J. Duties of the priests and Levites (18:1-32)
   K. Laws of purification (19:1-22)
   L. The Israelites leave Kadesh (20:1-29)

BBC

VOLUME 3

NUMBERS and DEUTERONOMY

Lynne M. Deming

ABINGDON PRESS
Nashville

Numbers and Deuteronomy

Copyright © 1988 by Graded Press

This book is printed on recycled, acid-free paper.

Library of Congress Cataloging-in-Publication Data

Cokesbury basic Bible commentary.
    Basic Bible commentary / by Linda B. Hinton . . . [et al.].
      p. cm.
    Originally published: Cokesbury basic Bible commentary. Nashville: Graded Press, © 1988.
    ISBN 0-687-02620-2 (pbk. : v. 1 : alk. paper)
    1. Bible—Commentaries. I. Hinton, Linda B. II. Title.
    [BS491.2.C65   1994]
    220.7—dc20
                                         94-10965
                                              CIP

ISBN-13: 978-0-687-02622-7 (v. 3, Numbers-Deuteronomy)
ISBN 0-687-02622-9 (v. 3, Numbers–Deuteronomy)
ISBN 0-687-02620-2 (v. 1, Genesis)
ISBN 0-687-02621-0 (v. 2, Exodus–Leviticus)
ISBN 0-687-02623-7 (v. 4, Joshua–Ruth)
ISBN 0-687-02624-5 (v. 5, 1–2 Samuel)
ISBN 0-687-02625-3 (v. 6, 1–2 Kings)
ISBN 0-687-02626-1 (v. 7, 2 Chronicles)
ISBN 0-687-02627-X (v. 8, Ezra–Esther)
ISBN 0-687-02628-8 (v. 9, Job)
ISBN 0-687-02629-6 (v. 10, Psalms)
ISBN 0-687-02630-X (v. 11, Proverbs–Song of Solomon)
ISBN 0-687-02631-8 (v. 12, Isaiah)
ISBN 0-687-02632-6 (v. 13, Jeremiah–Lamentation)
ISBN 0-687-02633-4 (v. 14, Ezekiel–Daniel)
ISBN 0-687-02634-2 (v. 15, Hosea–Jonah)
ISBN 0-687-02635-0 (v. 16, Micah–Malachi)
ISBN 0-687-02636-9 (v. 17, Matthew)
ISBN 0-687-02637-7 (v. 18, Mark)
ISBN 0-687-02638-5 (v. 19, Luke)
ISBN 0-687-02639-3 (v. 20, John)
ISBN 0-687-02640-7 (v. 21, Acts)
ISBN 0-687-02642-3 (v. 22, Romans)
ISBN 0-687-02643-1 (v. 23, 1–2 Corinthians)
ISBN 0-687-02644-X (v. 24, Galatians–Ephesians)
ISBN 0-687-02645-8 (v. 25, Philippians–2 Thessalonians)
ISBN 0-687-02646-6 (v. 26, 1 Timothy–Philemon)
ISBN 0-687-02647-4 (v. 27, Hebrews)
ISBN 0-687-02648-2 (v. 28, James–Jude)
ISBN 0-687-02649-0 (v. 29, Revelation)
ISBN 0-687-02650-4 (complete set of 29 vols.)

06 07 08 09 10 11 12 13–10 9 8 7 6 5 4 3

MANUFACTURED IN THE UNITED STATES OF AMERICA

Deuteronomy

Introduction to Numbers

The book of Numbers is the fourth book in the series often called "the five books of Moses" (Genesis–Deuteronomy). Numbers continues the historical narrative that began at Exodus 1:1.

In the original Hebrew, the name of this book is actually *In the wilderness* (NRSV) or *desert* (NIV). This name fits the contents of the book well, since the book of Numbers narrates events during the time of the Israelites' wilderness wanderings. The English title, Numbers, was given to this book because its earliest words have to do with the numbers of people in the census taken by Moses (chapter 1).

The Content of the Book

The book of Numbers may be divided into three parts: (1) the Israelites prepare to depart from Mount Sinai, chapters 1–10; (2) the Israelites journey to Kadesh, chapters 11–21; and (3) the Israelites approach the land of Canaan, chapters 22–36.

Numbers 1 continues the narrative that began in the book of Exodus. The people of Israel have left Egypt, journeyed to Sinai, and are receiving instructions about life and worship in the Promised Land. These instructions begin with the Ten Commandments (Exodus 19–20), and continue through the tenth chapter of Numbers, when the people finally pull up stakes and continue their journey to the Promised Land.

The Date of Numbers

The book of Numbers is part of the Pentateuch, or the five books of Moses. This group of narratives was written over a period of many years (900–500 B.C.) and was compiled in its final form sometime during the Exile.

Major Themes in Numbers

Theological themes in Numbers include the people's murmuring against Moses while they were wandering in the wilderness, God's continued presence with them during this time, the people's disobedience and lack of trust in God, and what the covenant relationship promises the people and what it requires of them.

PART ONE

Numbers 1–2

Introduction to These Chapters

The name *Numbers* is a fitting title for this book, since right at its beginning, in chapter 1, God commands Moses to number the people. In chapters 1 and 2, Moses numbers all the people of Israel except the Levites, and the arrangements are given for how the people are to be located when they encamp and when they march. In both these sections, the people of Israel are classified by tribes.

Here is an outline of chapters 1 and 2.
I. Moses Takes a Census (1:1-54)
   A. Introduction (1:1-16)
   B. The tribes are counted (1:17-46)
   C. Responsibilities of the Levites (1:47-54)
II. The Position of the Camps (2:1-34)
   A. The camp of Judah (2:1-9)
   B. The camp of Reuben (2:10-16)
   C. The camp of the Levites (2:17)
   D. The camp of Ephraim (2:18-24)
   E. The camp of Dan (2:25-31)
   F. Conclusion (2:32-34)

Introduction (1:1-16)

In Exodus 20 Moses had received rules and regulations for the religious life of the people of Israel. The book of Leviticus describes how these rules and regulations were made more specific, and shows Israel's cultic worship taking shape. Here in Numbers we turn to more political matters—regulations for how the people are to live together as twelve tribes.

In contrast to the receiving of the Ten Commandments in Exodus 20, where he is standing on top of a mountain, here Moses receives his instructions from God while he is inside the tent of meeting, in the wilderness of Sinai. The date is given based on the beginning of the Exodus from Egypt (see Exodus 19:1). According to the present passage, God speaks to Moses one year and one month after the people escaped from Egypt.

According to Exodus 40:1, the *tent of meeting* had been erected exactly one month before.

God tells Moses to take a census of all the congregation. God had given a similar command earlier, in Exodus 30:11-16. In the Exodus account, the census was for economic purposes—each person was to contribute a certain amount to the common treasury. Here in the Numbers account, however, the census is for military purposes. All males old enough to bear arms are to be counted.

The males in Israel are to be counted according to families, or fathers' houses. Each of the twelve tribes contained a certain number of families, which, in turn, contained a certain number of fathers' houses, or immediate families. The total number given for each tribe later in the chapter is the sum of the immediate families within the tribe.

According to verse 5, one male from each tribe is to represent the tribe in the census-taking. These twelve "assistants" to Moses would, of course, be necessary in order to count the large number of persons in Israel at that time. That task was too large for Moses and Aaron to accomplish unassisted.

In the verses that follow, one man from each tribe is listed, along with a designation of his immediate family. The tribe of Levi is left out, however; its situation is described in verses 47-54 of this chapter. In place of Levi,

NUMBERS AND DEUTERONOMY

the tribe of Joseph is divided into two parts, represented by Joseph's sons Ephraim and Manasseh. In this way, the number of tribes still equals twelve.

In all probability the list of heads of tribes that we have in verses 5-15 is an older list inserted by the writer at this point in the narrative. Several of the names on this list contain the stem *Ammi*, which is seen often as a name (or part of a name) in texts found at the ancient site of Mari, in Mesopotamia. If this list is older than the book of Numbers, then the persons listed probably had more important tasks than just assisting in the numbering for this census. Possibly they were chiefs representing their tribes in some sort of political organization.

The Tribes Are Counted (1:17-46)

According to verse 18, the census was undertaken and completed on the same day it was commanded by God—the first day of the second month.

Verses 20-46 summarize the information gathered from the census. The same formula is used to indicate the numbering for each tribe. In verse 46 the sum total is given: 603,550. This figure is a little larger than the one given in Numbers 26:51, where another census is taken to arrive at the total of 601,730.

Commentators have consistently questioned the number listed in verse 46, stating that it is too high to be realistic, given the land area and conditions in the Sinai wilderness. At least five explanations are possible.

(1) The number given includes women and children, although the text says that males who are able to go to war are to be the only ones counted. Even if the number includes women and children, it is still large enough to be questionable. That many people would have a difficult time moving on a wilderness journey together.

(2) The number is exaggerated to give a positive impression of the strength of the Israelites at that time.

(3) The number is correct, and we simply cannot

explain how so many persons could travel together at one time. (If there were 603,550 men, adding the women and children to the company would make the grand total greater than two million.)

(4) The number designations are based on some formula we do not understand. Often in ancient Hebrew, letters are used to represent numbers. In this passage, the writer has used some sort of code that we have no way to decipher.

(5) The word translated *thousand*, that is used to designate each subtotal, means something like a tribe, or unit, or troop. The words *thousand* and *hundred* may have been used in this way to designate military units (see Numbers 31:14). If *thousand* meant unit, then, for example, verse 21 would mean forty-six units; 500 men. Translating each subtotal in this way would produce a grand total of 5,550.

Responsibilities of the Levites (1:47-54)

These verses explain why the Levites were not numbered as part of the group of males able to go to war. The Levites are in charge of priestly matters, mainly involving the ark of the covenant. In verse 50, the ark is called *the tabernacle of the testimony* (NIV) or *covenant* (NRSV), referring to its contents, the tablets containing the law (law is sometimes called *testimony*).

According to verse 51, the Levites are the only ones allowed to even touch the ark. Anyone else who touches it will die. This law is reflected in the story in 2 Samuel 6, where David is returning the ark to Jerusalem and Uzzah dies because he touches the ark to stabilize it while in transit.

Whereas each of the twelve tribes has a specified place to be located while Israel is encamped, the Levites must encamp surrounding the ark, wherever it is located.

Verse 54 concludes the chapter by reminding the

reader that God had commanded all these arrangements, and Moses carried them out.

The Camp of Judah (2:1-9)

This description of the arrangement of the encampments contains both religious and military elements. Each group of three tribes has its own position, and all the tribes are arranged around the central position of the tent of meeting, which contains the ark. In this way, the presence of God in the midst of the people is symbolized.

The tribe of Judah, which is the largest, according to the list given in the previous chapter, has the most prominent position east of the tent of meeting. The east side is toward the sunrise (verse 3). According to verses 5-8, the *standard* (NIV) or the *regimental encampment* (NRSV; flag) of the camp of Judah included the tribes of Issachar and Zebulun as well.

The Camp of Reuben (2:10-16)

The camp of Reuben includes the tribes of Simeon and Gad as well. According to these verses, these three tribes occupy the space to the south. Notice that beginning from the east, the writer moves in a clockwise direction around the central location of the ark. This second group of three tribes is to start out second when Israel sets out on a march.

The Camp of the Levites (2:17)

The Levites occupy a special position in the arrangement. They are to be in the center, meaning that they are well-insulated from the outside. That position is fitting for the Levites, since they are to accompany the ark of the covenant at all times.

The Camp of Ephraim (2:18-24)

Moving clockwise, the camp of Ephraim (including the

tribes of Ephraim, Manasseh, and Benjamin) is to occupy the position on the west side of the center. Ephraim and Manasseh together are sometimes listed in place of the single tribe of Joseph, their father. This division is made to bring the total number of tribes to twelve, since the Levites are sometimes not listed. Sometimes Ephraim is listed first, as here (see Genesis 48:13-14), and sometimes Manasseh is listed first (see Numbers 26:28, for example).

The camp of Ephraim is to set out third in the marching order, according to verse 24.

The Camp of Dan (2:25-31)

The camp of Dan includes the tribes of Dan, Asher, and Naphtali. They are located on the northern side of the center, and are to set out fourth in the marching order.

Note that these three tribes are also located in the vicinity of one another when the land is allotted to the tribes (see Joshua 19:24-48). However, their location here in Numbers is according to ancient tribal lists, and not according to their later land allotments. That they are neighbors in both instances is probably coincidental.

Conclusion (2:32-34)

Verse 32 summarizes the numbering that was described in chapter 1. The total number given here is the same as the number given in 1:46. Verse 33 reiterates the fact that the Levites were not included in the census, according to God's command.

Verse 34 is another summary statement; this verse summarizes the information given in chapter 2. The language used here is reminiscent of the narrative in Genesis 1, mainly because of its repetitive nature. Most likely this material early in the book of Numbers comes from the same writer who wrote portions of the book of Genesis, including chapter 1.

§ § § § § § §

The Message of Numbers 1–2

These chapters introduce us to a very important phase in the history of the Israelites. The wilderness experience was formative for the Hebrew faith. Although the people do not actually set out on their journey until chapter 10, in these early chapters we see how they begin their preparations. What can we learn about God and God's relationship to the people?

§ God is with the people from beginning to end. The book of Numbers begins with the words *The* LORD *spoke,* setting the stage for what will happen in the rest of the book.

§ Moses and Aaron, along with the heads of each tribe, do not hesitate to do what God asks. They fulfill God's command on the same day it is given.

§ Those in charge of the religious dimension of Israelite life are set apart from the rest of the people. They are not counted among those persons able to bear arms.

§ There is an organized quality about the life of the Israelites during their time in the wilderness. This organization is under the leadership of God, through Moses.

§ § § § § § §

Numbers 3–6

Introduction to These Chapters

In these four chapters, the Israelites are still preparing
for their wilderness journey. Since the Levites were
excluded from the census taken in chapter 1, they are
counted by themselves in chapters 3 and 4. Other
material in this section includes laws concerning such
matters as adultery and living as a Nazirite.

Here is an outline of these chapters.
  I. The Duties of the Levites (3:1-51)
    A. Introduction (3:1-4)
    B. The leadership of Aaron (3:5-10)
    C. The Levites belong to God (3:11-13)
    D. The census of the Levites (3:14-39)
    E. A second census (3:40-51)
 II. A Third Census Is Taken (4:1-49)
    A. Instructions about the tent of meeting (4:1-33)
    B. Results of the census (4:34-49)
III. Laws and Instructions (5:1–6:21)
    A. The sanctity of the camp (5:1-4)
    B. Law concerning restitution (5:5-10)
    C. Law concerning adultery (5:11-31)
    D. Nazirite law (6:1-21)
 IV. Aaron's Blessing on the People (6:22-27)

Introduction (3:1-4)

In these introductory verses the names of the sons of
Aaron are given. These names are also listed in Exodus

6:23-25, where the heads of tribes are given. The fate of Nadab and Abihu, Aaron's elder sons, is described in Leviticus 10:1-7; they were slain for making an improper offering to God. According to verse 4 in this section, Nadab and Abihu died before they had any children to carry on their line.

The two remaining sons, Eleazar and Ithamar, were *anointed*—that is, installed as priests. The last part of verse 4 explains that Aaron, their father, is the high priest in charge of all other priests.

The Leadership of Aaron (3:5-10)

This section begins as a kind of second introduction to the larger section dealing with the Levites (chapters 3–4). According to God's command, the tribe of Levi is to minister to Aaron. This command sets Aaron aside as representative of the whole priesthood. All Levites are to be under his leadership.

The Levites are also responsible to the sons of Aaron, according to verse 9. Exodus 28:1-5 sets aside Aaron and his sons as a special group responsible for priestly duties in the tabernacle.

They shall *be put to death* (verse 10) echoes the thought of Numbers 1:51.

The Levites Belong to God (3:11-13)

Background for this section can be found in Exodus 34:19-20, which details the idea that the firstborn of everything belongs to God.

When I killed (NRSV) or *When I struck down* (NIV) (verse 13) refers to the consecration of the firstborn after the Israelite exodus from Egypt. See the reference in Exodus 13:2.

Sacrifice of human firstborn children, although it may have been practiced in the surrounding Canaanite culture, is never mentioned in the Old Testament as a practice of the Israelites. Instead, the Levites are a substitute for the firstborn; they are dedicated to God.

The Census of the Levites (3:14-39)

This section is a longer version of 1:47-54, where the Levites' status is first explained. The directions given in verse 14 are the same as those given for the census of the other tribes in chapter 1, except that those Levites to be counted are males who are one month old and upward (rather than those able to bear arms; see 1:3).

Verse 15 reflects the high mortality rate among infants in early Israel. Parents could be relatively certain of the survival of a child only after he or she had lived at least one month outside the womb.

According to this section, there were three main families among the Levites: the Gershonites, the Kohathites, and the Merarites. Each of these sons, Gershon, Kohath, and Merari, had two or more sons who formed subfamilies. This same list of the sons of Levi can be found in Exodus 6:16-19.

In verses 21-39, specific duties are given to each family as well as the location for where the family is to encamp. The Gershonites are responsible for the tent covering, the screen for the tent door, the hangings of the court, and the screen for the door of the court (see also Exodus 26–27). They are to encamp on the west side of the tabernacle.

The Kohathites are responsible for the holy objects, such as the ark, the table for the bread of the Presence, the lampstand, the sanctuary vessels, and the screen (which is the veil that separates the Holy of Holies where the ark is located). The Kohathites are to encamp on the south side of the tabernacle.

The Merarites, who encamp on the north side of the tabernacle, are responsible for its structural aspects (such as pillars and bases).

The sons of Moses and Aaron (verses 38-39) have the most important responsibilities—the rituals and rites of the sanctuary. Because of their importance relative to the other groups, the sons of Moses and Aaron encamp on the east side of the tabernacle.

Verse 38 reiterates 1:51 and 3:10.

This section is concluded in verse 39, where the total number of Levites one month and upward is given. The total number of men in the Levite tribe is significantly lower than the totals for the other tribes given in chapter 1. This is all the more remarkable because, in the case of the Levites, all males are counted, not just those who are old enough to bear arms (twenty years).

Although verse 39 gives the total as 22,000, the actual number of Kohathites (8,600), Gershonites (7,500), and Merarites (6,200) is 22,300.

A Second Census (3:40-51)

In contrast to the first census, described in chapter 1, in this one Moses is instructed to count all the firstborn males one month old and older. So this census is not for military purposes. Verse 41 explains the reasoning of verses 11-13 in more detail. The writer explains that the Levites are to substitute for the firstborn of all humans, and the cattle of the Levites are to substitute for the firstborn cattle of the Israelites.

In verse 43 the number of firstborn males in Israel is listed as 22,273—273 more than the number given for the Levites in verse 39. However, this number is closer to the actual number of Levites, which was 22,300. As with the numbers given for the tribes in chapter 1, this number seems difficult to understand. If it is related to the total number of Israelites given in 1:46 (603,550), each family in Israel would have somewhere in between forty and fifty children. As in chapter 1, the writer seems to be using some numeric formula that we can no longer decipher.

In verse 46, God explains that the 273 men over and above the original number of 22,000 need to be redeemed, because the substitution of Levites for firstborn Israelites is supposed to be one for one. For the 273 extra men, five shekels apiece are to be paid to the priest—a total of 1,365 shekels.

A shekel of the sanctuary (verse 47) was apparently different from a regular shekel, perhaps heavier.

Instructions About the Tent of Meeting (4:1-33)

In this section, more instructions are given about the Levites' duties (as in 3:21-37). Each family (the Gershonites, the Kohathites, and the Merarites) is counted and given special duties. This time, all males between the ages of thirty and fifty are counted, because those are the years of service in the tabernacle. (However, Numbers 8:23-24 gives the lower age as twenty-five; perhaps these verses come from another tradition).

The Kohathites occupy a special place within the tribe of Levi, since they are in charge of the holy things (see 3:27-32). As a result, they are counted and instructed first. However, their importance only extends so far, for they are not to touch or see the holy things. They are only allowed to carry the holy things while the Israelites are on the march. Aaron and his sons are the ones to dismantle and pack these things when the camp is moved.

The shielding (NIV) or *screening shield* (NRSV) (verse 5) is the material that separates the Holy of Holies from the rest of the tabernacle. In transit, this veil is placed over the ark so the contents will not be visible.

Verse 7 specifies that the bread of the Presence is to remain on the table at all times, even while the tabernacle is in transit.

According to verse 16, Eleazar, one of the sons of Aaron, has special responsibilities regarding the Kohathites. Verses 17-20 reiterate a special warning to the Kohathites, since they are the ones designated to carry the holy things and would have the greatest chance of touching or seeing them by mistake.

Verses 21-28 give the duties of the Gershonites, and

repeat the information given in 3:25-26. Aaron's son Ithamar is in charge of the Gershonites (verse 28), just as Eleazar is in charge of the Kohathites.

Verses 29-33 discuss the Merarites, giving the same instructions that were given in 3:36-37. Ithamar is in charge of the Merarites as well as the Gershonites.

Results of the Census (4:34-49)

In verse 34, the instructions given in verse 2 are carried out. Again, those from 30 to 50 years of age are counted, indicating that the years of service in the tabernacle are the significant factor in this census. The same formula is used in each case: 2,750 Kohathites are counted; 2,630 Gershonites are counted; and 3,200 Merarites are counted. The total given here is 8,580, compared to the total of 22,000 Levites one month old and upward, given in 3:39.

The Sanctity of the Camp (5:1-4)

According to these verses, three types of people are excluded from the camp because they are unclean in some way. (Verse 3 indicates that these persons may be either male or female.) Lepers are to be excluded; see the laws regarding lepers in Leviticus 13. Specifically, Leviticus 13:46 indicates that lepers are to be located in a special place outside the city.

Also to be excluded from the camp are those with a bodily discharge (see Leviticus 15), and those who have physical contact with the dead (see Leviticus 21). In verse 4 this command is carried out. According to Deuteronomy 23:10-15, Israel had strict rules for cleanness inside the camp.

Law Concerning Restitution (5:5-10)

As background for this section, refer to Leviticus 6:1-7.

Verse 8 adds a new element to the law found in Leviticus 6. Here the restitution money goes to the priest if the wronged person does not have a relative to whom restitution can be made; it does not merely remain unpaid.

Verse 8 also states that in reality the sum is paid to God; it just goes through the priest. Apparently this regulation assumes that the wronged person has become dependent on a kinsman, either legally or economically.

Verses 9-10 are more general, in that they instruct the people to bring all offerings to the priest, to whom they then belong.

Law Concerning Adultery (5:11-31)

Other laws concerning adultery are found elsewhere in the Old Testament (Leviticus 20:10, for example), but here the difference is that there are no witnesses. *She was not caught in the act* (verse 13) means that no one saw her. However, her husband may become suspicious (have feelings of jealousy). This law provides a way for the husband to bring the wife before God for a judgment, since there is no way for a human decision to be made.

Verses 16-28 describe the trial that would take place if the woman were brought before God. The water of bitterness (verse 18) indicates the potential of a negative judgment upon the woman. After some preliminary preparations, the woman must take *the oath of the curse* (NRSV) or *the curse of the oath* (NIV) (verse 21), but her words are not supplied in the text.

In verses 23-28 the woman is forced to drink the water of bitterness. If she is guilty, then the water will cause her great pain and all will realize her guilt. If she is not guilty, when she drinks the water she will experience no pain and will (later) be able to bear children. And, everyone will know that she is innocent of the crime of which she was accused.

Verses 29-31 conclude the section by repeating what was stated earlier. Although this text does not specify what the punishment would be if the woman were found guilty, it would have been stoning for both the man and the woman (see Deuteronomy 22:21-22). If the woman is found innocent, however, the man is presumably not punished for the trouble and humiliation he has caused his wife.

NUMBERS AND DEUTERONOMY

Nazirite Law (6:1-21)

The word *Nazirite* means one separated, or one consecrated. There are several examples of Nazirites in the Old Testament; the most famous example is Samson (see Judges 13:5). According to verse 2, either men or women could be Nazirites.

Although no specific role is assigned to those who decide to be Nazirites, there were several rules to be obeyed by persons who joined the sect. First, they were to drink no wine or strong drink (verses 3-4). Abstinence from alcoholic beverages separated the Nazirites from the surrounding Canaanite culture, which was dependent on wine for religious and other aspects of its existence.

Second, Nazirites were not to cut their hair. Cutting the hair symbolized an invasion of personal integrity. And third, Nazirites were to have no contact with the dead, making them unclean. This same rule applied to the priests as well (see Leviticus 21).

Verses 9-12 give instructions about accidental contact with the dead, since it would have been easy to walk into a room without realizing it contained a dead body.

Verses 13-20 detail what was to happen at the end of the consecration period. Verse 21 concludes the section by stating that taking the Nazirite vow does not remove other responsibilities for vows and offerings that persons may have.

Aaron's Blessing on the People (6:22-27)

According to Deuteronomy 21:5, blessing is part of the duties assigned to the priests.

The emphasis is on the fact that God is the one really doing the blessing; *The LORD* is repeated at the beginning of each of three lines.

Make his face to shine (verse 25) means showing a kind of benevolence to the people (see also Psalm 31:16).

And give you peace (verse 26) refers to a sense of wholeness or well-being (see also Psalm 44:3).

§ § § § § § §

The Message of Numbers 3–6

In these chapters, the people of Israel are still preparing for their wilderness journey that they will undertake beginning in chapter 10. In this section we read about everything from a census to rules and regulations regarding life in community. What can we learn about God and about God's chosen people from the material in these chapters?

§ Ever since Israel's earliest days, certain people have been set apart by God as having religious responsibilities and a special relationship to God.

§ God can make demands and expect obedience to those demands.

§ Living in community required a certain amount of organization, including designated leaders and rules that must be followed for order to be maintained.

§ Wherever the people went in their wilderness journey, God was with them.

§ § § § § § §

Numbers 7–9

Introduction to These Chapters

This section of the book of Numbers contains a tribe-by-tribe listing of offerings brought by tribal leaders to the service of dedication of the tabernacle, a service of consecration for the Levites, who have the priestly responsibilities in the tabernacle, and further preparations for the wilderness journey. This is the last section that describes preparation for the journey. At the end of chapter 9 (actually, at 10:11), the Israelites set out on their journey through the wilderness.

Here is an outline of Numbers 7–9.
 I. Consecration of the Tabernacle (7:1-89)
    A. The leaders arrive in wagons (7:1-9)
    B. The dedication of the altar (7:10-89)
 II. Consecration of the Levites (8:1-26)
    A. The lighting of the lamps (8:1-4)
    B. The ceremony of purification (8:5-22)
    C. The Levites' duties are assigned (8:23-26)
 III. Miscellaneous Laws (9:1–10:10)
    A. Laws concerning the Passover (9:1-14)
    B. The departure from Sinai (9:15–10:10)

The Leaders Arrive in Wagons (7:1-9)
The date mentioned at the beginning of this chapter (the day when Moses had finished setting up the tabernacle) has already passed (see Exodus 40:17).

Perhaps this section was a later addition to the narrative, or was placed in the wrong location by a later editor.

On this day, the leaders of the twelve tribes brought offerings to God—six wagons (one for every two tribes) and twelve oxen (one per tribe). The writer does not indicate what, if anything, is contained in these wagons or on these oxen. Apparently, the wagons and the oxen are themselves the offering.

Note the repetitive language in verse 3; this section was probably written by the same writer who wrote Numbers 1, Genesis 1, and other similar texts in the early portion of the Old Testament.

In verse 5, God commands Moses to give the wagons and oxen to the Levites, to be used in transporting the furnishings of the tabernacle. In carrying out this command, Moses gives Gershon two wagons and four oxen; he gives Merari four wagons and eight oxen; and he gives nothing to Kohath. Because the Kohathites are responsible for carrying the holy things while the Israelites are marching, they must use their shoulders rather than wagons or oxen.

The Dedication of the Altar (7:10-89)

In this rather lengthy section, the offerings the tribal leaders bring for the dedication of the altar are enumerated. Verse 11 introduces what follows with God's command that one offering be brought each day for twelve days, with a different tribal leader coming forward each day.

As background for this section, refer to Leviticus 9, where the guidelines for this offering are given. According to Leviticus 9:3-4, the people are to offer a goat, a calf, a lamb, an ox, a ram, and a cereal offering for the dedication of the altar. Here, however, the offerings are much more elaborate. Possibly these are two independent traditions about what happened when the sanctuary was first dedicated. Or perhaps the writer of

NUMBERS AND DEUTERONOMY

Numbers 7 thought the earlier offerings mentioned in Leviticus were not elaborate enough.

The order of appearance of the tribal leaders in verses 12-83 follows the order of the encampments in Numbers 2. Each tribal leader brings exactly the same offering, and this list is repeated twelve times.

Verses 84-88 summarize the offerings and give the totals. Verse 89 is difficult to interpret. At first glance it reads like an introduction to a new speech that Moses will deliver after hearing it from the Lord. However, the writer has not provided the actual speech. Or perhaps the writer merely intends to indicate by these words that God has received the offerings brought by the tribal leaders.

The Lighting of the Lamps (8:1-4)

These verses describe the lighting of the lamps in the tabernacle, which is the responsibility of the priests, the sons of Aaron. Background for this section can be found in Exodus 25, where the seven-branched lampstand is described in detail (see verses 31-40). The seven (detachable) lamps are to be placed in such a way that the light they give off shines in front of the lampstand.

The Ceremony of Purification (8:5-22)

In verse 5, God commands a special purification ceremony to take place for the Levites. As the first step in this purification ceremony, the Levites are to be cleansed, a procedure that has three parts. First, water of expiation will be sprinkled on them. Expiation indicates the purifying effect of this water. Then, they are to shave their bodies with razors. And third, they are to wash their clothes and themselves.

In order to approach the sanctuary, the Levites must bring sacrifices: they must bring both a cereal offering and a sin offering.

According to verse 10, when the Levites have finished

these preparations, the people of Israel will lay their hands on the Levites, signifying that the Levites are truly a substitute for their own first-born; they are dedicated to God.

Verse 11 says that the Levites will be offered before the Lord as a *wave* (NIV or *elevation* (NRSV) *offering.* Wave offerings were those that were waved back and forth in front of the altar, symbolizing the offering of the sacrifice to God and the receiving of a portion of that offering. In this context, the wave offering of the Levites symbolizes the fact that the Levites belong to Aaron just as the wave offerings belong to the priests.

In verse 14, after the proper preparations have been made, the Levites are ready to enter the tent and perform their assigned duties. Verses 15-22 repeat what has been narrated in the previous verses, with a summary statement in verse 22.

The Levites' Duties Are Assigned (8:23-25)

This section relates to Numbers 4:2-4, which also gives the age limitations for the Levites' service in the tabernacle. Here, however, the minimum age is given as twenty-five, not thirty as in the Numbers 4 passage. The upper limit is the same in both passages, although the present passage seems to offer some flexibility. The Levites, after the age of fifty, can still minister to each other inside the tent, but cannot perform any official functions.

The comparatively short length of service for the Levites (twenty to twenty-five years) indicates that this responsibility requires the maturity that comes with age.

Laws Concerning the Passover (9:1-14)

According to verse 1, the date for this passage is the same as that of Exodus 40:17, and is earlier than the date given in Numbers 1:1 (on the first day of the second month of the second year). See the note on Numbers 7:1.

This section is concerned with additional rules and regulations regarding the Passover celebration. When the commemoration is prevented for any reason, it will take place exactly one month later (in the second month on the fourteenth day in the evening).

Two legitimate reasons are given for missing the Passover celebration, held on the first month, the fourteenth day. First, the example is mentioned of several men who are unclean from contact with a dead body. They ask why they cannot keep the Passover. Moses refers the question to God, and receives an answer in verses 9-14. Yes, they can keep the Passover, but they must wait for one month.

Second, those who have been on a journey can keep the Passover one month later as well. However, verse 13 warns that in order to postpone the Passover celebration for a month there must be a good reason. Persons who do not have a legitimate reason for postponing the celebration will be cut off from their people, that is, put to death.

Verse 14 adds that strangers can also celebrate the Passover, as long as the proper rules and regulations are observed.

The Departure from Sinai (9:15–10:10)

This section is divided into two main parts: (1) a description of the cloud and fire that symbolize God's presence with the Israelites (verses 15-23), and (2) the making of the trumpets that will be used both for practical and for cultic purposes (verses 1-10).

Exodus 40:34-38 gives a similar description of the cloud and fire symbolizing God's presence at the tabernacle. Cloud and fire are common elements in a theophany, or manifestation of God's presence. God's presence was manifested in a similar way when the Israelites left Egypt by night (see Exodus 13:21-22).

Verses 1-10 describe the making of the silver trumpets

that will be used for summoning the congregation and for breaking camp. Two trumpets are made, and when both are blown together the people are to gather at the entrance of the tabernacle. If only one trumpet is blown, then only the leaders of the people are to gather.

According to verse 6, the first group of tribes to leave when the camp is broken are those located on the east side of the tabernacle. Those on the south side are to leave next. Nothing is said about the other two groups, however.

In verse 7 two different sounds of the trumpet are described. The trumpets can be blown, signifying that it is time for the people (or the leaders) to gather. Or an alarm can be sounded, signifying that it is time for the congregation to set out on a march. According to verse 8, the sons of Aaron have the responsibility for sounding the trumpets.

Verse 10 mentions another, cultic function for these trumpets. They are to be sounded on the first days of feasts, which commonly take place on the first days of months.

The Message of Numbers 7–9

§ These chapters contain the final preparations the people of Israel made before they left Mount Sinai. What can we learn from this material about God and about God's relationships with the chosen people?

§ Certain persons in Israel were set apart by God for special services.

§ God expects and requires a certain portion in return for what God does on behalf of the people.

§ God is the ultimate source of authority about rules and regulations of Israel's life and faith.

§ Israelites and sojourners alike can participate in the feasts and festivals of Israelite faith.

§ God's presence abides with the Israelites while they journey through the wilderness.

§ § § § § § §

Numbers 10–12

Introduction to These Chapters

Here the Israelites begin their march, journeying in the wilderness for the next forty years. The section opens with a description of all the last-minute preparations. So many people embarking on a journey at the same time, accompanied by the presence of God, must have been an impressive sight. The contrast is vivid when, immediately after they set out, the people begin murmuring against Moses. They are unhappy, and their unhappiness results in dissension among the leaders.

Here is an outline of these chapters.
  I. The Israelites Journey to Kadesh (10:11-36)
      A. Introduction (10:11-12)
      B. The order of march (10:13-28)
      C. The Israelites set out (10:29-36)
 II. The Israelites Murmur in the Wilderness (11:1-35)
      A. The fire of the Lord (11:1-3)
      B. The people crave manna and meat (11:4-15)
      C. The leadership of Moses (11:16-30)
      D. The people eat meat (11:31-35)
III. Miriam Is Punished (12:1-16)
      A. Miriam and Aaron speak against Moses (12:1-8)
      B. Miriam becomes leprous (12:9-16)

Introduction (10:11-12)

The people of Israel have been building up to this moment for a long time. They first arrived in the wilderness of Sinai eleven months previously (see Exodus 19:1). There Moses received the Ten Commandments, and the people have been there ever since.

In chapter 2 of Numbers the people began their preparations to leave Sinai, and now, after 19 days, they are finally ready to set out. The date is the second month of the second year, on the twentieth day of the month. The cloud that is over the tabernacle represents the presence of God with the people as they travel.

Verse 12 indicates that the people travel in stages. According to Numbers 33, these stages began in Egypt. Numbers 33:15-16 indicates where the wilderness of Sinai is located among the stages that began when the people left Egypt under the leadership of Moses.

The first stopping place after leaving the wilderness of Sinai is the wilderness of Paran. No one knows for certain where Paran is located; probably it was an oasis somewhere in the southern Sinai peninsula.

The Order of March (10:13-28)

In this section, the tribes are listed in the order of their setting out on the wilderness journey. The order given here is the same as in chapter 2, where the arrangement of the encampments is given. Also, the names of the leaders are the same as in chapter 2.

According to verses 17 and 21, the tabernacle is dismantled in two separate operations before the march begins. The outer frame is taken down first, and then taken away by the Gershonites and the Merarites. In the second stage, the holy things are removed by the Kohathites, who then set out carrying them. In this way, when the Kohathites arrive at the new campsite they will find the tabernacle erected and ready for the holy things to be placed inside.

Verse 28 concludes the section by a summary statement. Again we see the repetitive nature of this writer's style.

The Israelites Set Out (10:29-36)

This section reads somewhat differently from what has preceded in chapters 1–10; it is in a more narrative style and is less repetitious. It contains two short vignettes, one about Moses and his father-in-law and one ancient tradition about the ark and its important role in the life of the Israelites while they journeyed.

According to verse 29, Hobab was the father-in-law of Moses. Elsewhere in the Old Testament Hobab is known as Jethro (see Exodus 3:1, for example). In verse 29, the phrases *Reuel the Midianite* and *Moses' father-in-law* stand beside each other in an uncertain relationship. One way to read this verse is that Hobab was actually the brother-in-law of Moses, not his father-in-law. However, such texts as Judges 4:11 indicate that Hobab was probably Moses' father-in-law, not the son of his father-in-law. Hobab was the priest of Midian and the son of a man named Reuel.

Moses asks Hobab to go with the Israelites on their journey to the land that God had promised them earlier. Hobab refuses, saying that he intends to go back to his own people. Verse 31 makes clear Moses' motivation in asking Hobab to go on the journey. Moses wants Hobab to guide the people through the wilderness; he is to be their eyes. If he agrees to perform this service, his reward will be a share in what has been promised to the people of Israel (which meant a portion of the Promised Land, although this is not stated specifically).

According to verse 33 Hobab changes his mind and decides to accompany the Israelites. Although the text does not state specifically that Hobab goes on the journey, we can assume from reading several passages in the book of Judges that Hobab remains among the Israelites at least for a while (see Judges 1:16; 4:11).

Verses 33-36 are an ancient tradition about the role of the sacred ark that accompanied the Israelites on their journey through the wilderness. Curiously, the ark was described in Exodus 25:10-22, and has not been mentioned since that time. According to the Exodus account, the ark was a portable wooden chest that rested inside the tabernacle, and above which God was invisibly seated. According to Deuteronomy 10:3, Moses made the ark himself, at the command of God.

Verse 33 does not say that the ark goes three days ahead of the people. Rather, the ark goes ahead, or in front of the people on their three days' journey. According to 10:21, the tabernacle, which contained the ark, always arrived first at the new camp.

Moses' words in verse 35 indicate that God's presence was thought to be in the ark. *Ten thousand thousands (NRSV) or countless thousands* (NIV) (verse 36) should not be taken literally. This phrase is a Hebrew expression used to indicate a large number of people.

The Fire of the Lord (11:1-3)

This introductory section is for the purpose of explaining how the place Taberah got its name. *Taberah* means *burning*. At the time the Israelites were journeying in the wilderness, there must have been a place somewhere in between Paran and Palestine, the Promised Land, that was called Taberah. However, we no longer know where it was.

The name *burning* came from the phenomenon of the fire of the Lord, which descended upon the Israelites as a result of their murmuring and complaining against Moses. Verse 1 in this section mentions this murmuring for the first time in the book of Numbers (see also Exodus 16:2-3; 17:3; Numbers 12:1-2; 14:2-3; and 21:4-5). Murmuring is a constant theme in the wilderness narratives.

The nature of the fire of the Lord is not explained; possibly it was lightning that struck the camp and caused it to catch on fire. Fortunately, the fire consumed only the outlying portions of the camp, and abated when Moses interceded on behalf of the people.

The People Crave Manna and Meat (11:4-15)

The *rabble* mentioned in verse 4 are also mentioned in Exodus 12:38, although there these people are called a *mixed crowd* (NRSV) or *many other people* (NIV). They are people of mixed origins who have attached themselves to the wandering Israelites, and they are the ones blamed for the strong craving for meat that causes so much trouble for the Hebrews during this time. Even though it is the rabble who first have the craving, their desire affects the Israelites as well, and they begin complaining and asking for meat.

Verse 4 says that the people wept again, a reference to the first time they complained, soon after they left Egypt (see Exodus 16:2-3). They remember the delicious food they ate in Egypt, and now they have only manna to eat. Earlier, in response to their complaints, God had provided manna when there was nothing to eat. Now, however, they are tired of the manna.

Manna is described in verses 7-9. This substance was described earlier in Exodus 16:31, but more detail is given here in the Numbers passage. The name apparently comes from the Hebrew word translated "What is it?" reflecting the people's question when they first saw the substance lying on the ground early one morning. According to verse 8, manna could be ground, beaten, or boiled before it was eaten.

Manna is of uncertain origin. Possibly it came from insects, or it could be a product of the tamarisk tree.

In verses 10-15, Moses complains to God that the people are a burden to him with their constant complaining. In fact, Moses goes so far as to ask God to kill him rather than forcing such a heavy burden upon him. Moses had made a similar speech in Exodus 17:4.

The Leadership of Moses (11:16-30)

This section begins with God's response to the request Moses has just made. Moses is to lighten his burden by gathering seventy elders into the tent of meeting, where God will place some of Moses' spirit of leadership upon them. This same suggestion was made earlier by Moses' father-in-law (Jethro, or Hobab); see Exodus 18:21-23.

The *spirit* mentioned first in verse 17 is the divine spirit which, when given to a human being, endows that person with charismatic leadership. Moses is already a charismatic leader; now he will share that leadership with others. In order to share leadership, Moses will have to share some of the divine spirit as well.

Verses 18-23 continue the narrative about the lack of food. God will answer the people's complaints and give them meat. In fact, they will have so much meat that they will become sick of it, just as they became sick of the manna when they were forced to eat so much of it.

In verses 21-22 Moses raises a very practical question. How can God feed 600,000 men (see also Exodus 12:37) meat for a whole month? God's answer comes in verse 23, in the form of a rhetorical question: Can't God do anything?

In verses 24-30 the story line returns to the seventy elders who will share Moses' leadership burden. God distributes the spirit among them, and they prophesy (see also 1 Samuel 10:6).

Verses 26-30 narrate the episode of the two elders who, for some reason, did not go to the tent of meeting to receive the spirit. Instead, they remained in the camp. This story assumes that the tent of meeting was located outside the camp (see also Exodus 33:7-11). This location is in contrast to the instructions given in Numbers 2, where the tent of meeting is to be located in the middle of the encampments. Possibly there are two traditions about the location of the tent of meeting that are intertwined throughout these narratives.

According to verse 26, these two elders, Eldad and Medad, were among those registered, that is, they were part of the community. For some unknown reason, however, they did not go to the tent of meeting. But their location did not prevent them from receiving the spirit at the same time the other seventy received it. And just as the others did, these two men immediately begin to prophesy.

The writer does not explain how the ability of these seventy elders to prophesy will help Moses with his burdens of leadership.

The People Eat Meat (11:31-35)

With these verses we return to the narrative about the provision of food in the wilderness. In answer to the people's request, God sends a wind that brings quails from the sea (the Gulf of Aqaba). Quails are common to that area; they migrate over the desert each spring and fall. Because they are large birds, they tire easily and fall to the ground to rest. When that happens, they are easily caught without the use of sophisticated equipment.

Verse 31 states that the birds are on the ground as far as a day's journey on this side and a day's journey on the other side, a total of two days' journey, or about 40-50 miles. They are two cubits above the ground, or about one yard deep. (One cubit is about eighteen inches, or the distance from the elbow to the end of the fingertip.)

According to verse 32, there are so many quails that it takes the people two days and one night to collect them all and spread them out to dry. Ten homers is the least amount gathered by anyone—about 89 bushels. Eating the quail causes the people to become sick very quickly, just as God had promised (see verse 20). Their illness symbolizes their lack of trust in Moses and God.

According to the note in verse 34, the name given to the place where these events took place symbolizes the craving that the people had there and that got them into serious difficulty. The name of the place means *graves of craving*.

Verse 35 summarizes the section and looks toward the

next section by indicating the location of the next stage in the people's journey.

Miriam and Aaron Speak Against Moses (12:1-8)

This whole chapter narrates Miriam's punishment for challenging Moses, and, by association, God. Two complaints are voiced by Miriam and Aaron in the first two verses: (1) that Moses married a Cushite woman (verse 1), and (2) that Moses claims a special relationship with God that is exclusive to him (verse 2).

The Cushite woman mentioned in verse 2 may be Zipporah (see Exodus 2:21), in which case the word Cushite was used here to include Midianite people and others as well. Or, perhaps Miriam and Aaron are referring to another wife who is not mentioned elsewhere in the Old Testament. The writer does not indicate why Miriam and Aaron object to this Cushite woman.

According to verse 2, Moses and Aaron complain that Moses thinks God speaks only through him. They raise the question of whether God ever speaks through anyone else (them, for example). After all, we know that Miriam was called a prophetess (see Exodus 15:20, for example). Aaron, however, does not make that claim for himself.

Moses does not have a chance to answer their complaint, for God intervenes quickly and calls all three to the tent of meeting to give a response. God comes down in a pillar of cloud and calls Miriam and Aaron to come forward to hear the response. Moses is left behind, although he probably can still hear what is going on.

Verses 6-8 give God's answer to the complaint about God's special relationship with Moses. (God does not respond to the complaint about Moses' wife, and Moses does not have a chance to answer, either.) God claims to make an exception in Moses' case, not speaking through a vision as was the case with other prophets. In Moses' case, God speaks directly to him in language he can understand (not dark speech which requires an interpretation). This special relationship should have made Miriam and Aaron afraid to confront Moses since they were, by extension, confronting God.

Miriam Becomes Leprous (12:9-16)

According to verse 9, God becomes angry with them, but only Miriam is punished. God leaves the tent of meeting, and, when the cloud disappears, Miriam is left leprous (white as snow). Aaron is still involved, however, and he pleads with Moses to remove the punishment, since they now recognize their foolishness. Moses, in turn, pleads with God to remove the punishment. God refuses, but agrees to reduce the days of exclusion from the camp to seven. This amount of time is at least equal to the punishment Miriam would have received if she had done something shameful enough to warrant her father's spitting in her face.

Miriam's exclusion from the camp requires the people to wait for her return before they could break camp and move on to their next location.

The geographical note in verse 16 is confusing, since the people had already come and gone from Paran, according to 10:12. Perhaps this is a different tradition in which they had not yet arrived in Paran. Or perhaps their time at Hazeroth (11:35) was a temporary stay in between longer encampments in the wilderness of Paran.

§ § § § § § §

The Message of Numbers 10–12

In these chapters, the people finally embark on their journey through the wilderness toward the Promised Land. Several important themes surface in these chapters, and will continue to appear throughout the wilderness journey.

§ All details of the journey are at the command of God, through Moses.

§ There is an orderedness about the journey that is also ordained by God and necessary to keep the people together in community on such a long and arduous trip.

§ God is present with the people as they depart, and remains with them throughout the journey.

§ God is willing to provide help to Moses as he chafes under the burden of leadership that has been given to him.

§ Greed and complaining bring punishment from God.

§ § § § § § §

Numbers 13–16

Introduction to These Chapters

In this section a group of spies among the camp undertake a reconnaissance mission to spy out the land of Canaan. After receiving advice to the contrary, the Israelites decide to attack anyway, and the results are disastrous. This section also contains some cultic regulations and a story about an uprising against Moses.

Here is an outline of Numbers 13–16.
  I. The Israelites Spy on Canaan (13:1-33)
      A. The spies are designated (13:1-16)
      B. Moses instructs the spies (13:17-24)
      C. The spies report (13:25-33)
 II. The Israelites Attack Canaan (14:1-45)
      A. The people respond to the report (14:1-10)
      B. Dialogue between Moses and God (14:11-38)
      C. The results of the attack (14:39-45)
III. Laws Concerning Offerings (15:1-41)
      A. Cereal and drink offerings (15:1-16)
      B. Offering of the first fruits (15:17-21)
      C. Laws concerning atonement (15:22-31)
      D. Penalty for violating the sabbath (15:32-36)
      E. The Israelites are to wear tassels (15:37-41)
 IV. Korah Rebels Against Moses (16:1-50)
      A. Korah and others revolt (16:1-15)
      B. Korah and others are punished (16:16-35)
      C. Appendix (16:36-50)

The Spies Are Designated (13:1-16)

In this section we have the first mention of a military conquest of the land of Canaan. The wanderings of the people have brought them to a location that is close enough to Canaan that Moses could send a group of spies to scout out the territory. (According to 12:16, they were currently encamped in the wilderness of Paran, somewhere in Sinai peninsula. Verse 17 says that Moses sends these spies to the Negeb, which is a desert area south of Canaan.)

Verses 1-3 introduce this section by indicating divine guidance. It is God who commands Moses to send these spies. According to verse 2, Moses is to send one man among the leadership of each of the twelve tribes. The wording of verse 2 seems to indicate that within each of Israel's tribes there was a core of leadership among whom leaders could be chosen for individual tasks.

The tribal designations are given in basically the same order as in Numbers 1:5-15, except that two pairs are reversed (Manasseh-Ephraim and Naphtali-Gad). The leaders designated here are not the same as those mentioned in chapter 1.

In verse 8 Joshua is called Hoshea for some reason; in verse 16 Moses changes his name to the more common Joshua. Note the language of the concluding statement in verse 16. We see the writer of the early chapters in Numbers at work again in this context.

Moses Instructs the Spies (13:17-24)

Verse 17 makes Moses' instructions more specific than in verse 1; here Moses instructs the men to spy out the Negeb. The Negeb is a desert region in the southern portion of the land of Canaan. In verses 18-20, the spies are instructed to see six things: (1) what the land is like, (2) what the people are like, (3) how many people live in the region, (4) whether the land is good or bad, (5) what the cities are like, and (6) how fertile the land is.

Verses 21-24 report twice that Moses' instructions are carried out (once in verse 21 and a second time in verses 22-24). The Wilderness of Zin (verse 21) is located on the southern border of the land of Canaan, east of Kadesh-barnea (see Joshua 15:3). The northern limits of the land are given as Rehob and the Entrance of Hamath, which are near the source of the Jordan River.

According to verses 22-24, the spies move northward to the city of Hebron through the desert. Verse 32 also mentions the descendants of Anak, or the Anakim. The word *Anak* means something like *necklace*, so these people were called the *necklace people*. They were known for their great size, which must have been intimidating to the Israelites.

The establishment of the city of Hebron is dated relative to the founding of Zoan (the Greek name for this city is Tanis). It was the Hyksos capital, built sometime around 1700 B.C. Near Hebron is the Valley of Eschol, known for the fertility of its land that produced large, juicy grapes. In fact, verse 23 indicates that these grape clusters were so large that they had to be laid on top of two poles and carried by two men.

The Spies Report (13:25-33)

The report of the spies to Moses, Aaron, and all the rest of the people is in two parts: the first part in verses 25-26 and the second part in verses 27-29. According to verse 25, they had been spying out the land for forty days.

Verse 26 mentions Kadesh. This site is the same as Kadesh-barnea, an oasis where the Israelites spent much of their time during the years of wilderness wandering. Kadesh was located between two wildernesses—the Wilderness of Paran and the Wilderness of Zin. It was about fifty miles southwest of Beersheba.

The men report that they found a land that flows with milk and honey (verse 27). *Milk and honey* represent foods pleasing to nomadic people as well as a land of fertility.

Milk and honey were used earlier to symbolize what the Promised Land would be like (see Exodus 3:8).

Verse 28 gives the bad news. The land that was spied out contains people who are large and strong, and these people live in cities that are large and well-fortified. The Anakim were alluded to earlier, in verse 22. Verse 29 lists the other inhabitants of Canaan besides these necklace people.

According to verse 30, the people in the congregation must have been distressed at what the spies had to say. Caleb assures the people that Canaan will be no problem to conquer.

The report in verses 32-33 repeats what was already said previously (see verse 28), but this second report adds the note that the Anakim were also known as *Nephilim*. We know of the Nephilim as the people called giants in Genesis 6:4. Tradition held that the Nephilim were unusually large people due to a divine-human marriage sometime earlier in their history.

The People Respond to the Report (14:1-10)

The initial response of the people to the spies' report was already alluded to in 13:30, but in 14:1-10 a more complete description is given. Upon hearing the news they immediately begin to weep. This response is similar to what happened earlier when the people were hungry for meat (see 11:10).

The rebellion of the congregation is first against Moses and Aaron (verse 2) and then against God (verse 3). Their words sound like their lament in Exodus 16:3, just after they had left Egypt. Apparently their distress is so great that they decide to appoint a leader to replace Moses, someone who will lead them back to Egypt where life was better. This request causes Moses and Aaron to fall on their faces in despair.

According to verses 6-7, Caleb and Joshua join forces to try to persuade the people that the spies' report should be disregarded (at least the negative aspects of this report). After all, they say, God will lead the people safely (verse 8) if it is God's will for them to be in the land of Canaan. The people who live in Canaan are not to be feared (according to Caleb and Joshua) because they will be like bread for the Israelites. In other words, the inhabitants of Canaan will be defeated just as easily as bread is eaten, because they do not have God's protection.

According to verse 10, the people would have stoned Caleb and Joshua if God had not intervened at that time. *The glory of the* LORD refers to a halo of light that surrounded God's presence, preventing people from witnessing the divine presence. According to tradition, no one except Moses could see the face of God without perishing (see Deuteronomy 34:10-12).

Dialogue Between Moses and God (14:11-38)

God responds to the people's defiance by punishing them severely. This section provides details about the reasons and about the judgment.

Verse 11 mentions the signs God had given the people earlier; these signs are manna and quails (see Chapter 11). In verse 12, God threatens to make a mightier nation than Israel, after striking Israel *with the pestilence* (NRSV) or *plague* (NIV) (that is, disease). God had made the same threat earlier (see Exodus 32:9-10, where God considers destroying the people and raising up another).

Verse 13 introduces the speech of Moses that ends at verse 19. Moses' speech includes an argument (verse 13-16) and a request for forgiveness (verses 17-19). According to Moses' argument, Egypt and other surrounding nations are keeping an eye on the Israelites to see what will happen to them after their deliverance from Egypt. If the Israelites are destroyed, these nations will hear about the destruction and will question God's power to bring about obedience on the part of the chosen people.

NUMBERS AND DEUTERONOMY

Verses 17-19 include an appeal to God's power (verse 17) and a quote from Exodus 34:6-7, which is an old ritual used to describe the power of Israel's God.

Verses 20-25 then give God's answer to Moses' request. According to verse 20, God's answer is yes. *I have forgiven* means God has repented, or changed an earlier decision. God repents of an earlier decision also in Exodus 32:14.

Verses 21-23 give the "however." As punishment for their faithlessness, none of the present generation will see the Promised Land. The one exception is Caleb, who is described as God's servant. Why is Caleb excepted? Because his spirit is *different* (see 13:30, where Caleb is the only one advocating entry into Canaan).

Verse 25 gives God's final instructions. In order to avoid the Amalekites and the Canaanites, the people should detour by way of the wilderness, which means doubling back and going up on the east side of the Jordan River.

God's response to Israel's faithlessness continues in verses 26-35. God raises the question of how long the people will murmur against Moses and God (see verse 27). The answer comes in verse 29—not very much longer. Everyone 20 years old and upward (that is, everyone who was numbered; see 1:1-3), will die in the wilderness. Caleb and Joshua are excepted. All the women who were twenty years old and upward were ignored. The children were spared (verse 31). But they still have to endure forty years in the wilderness, suffering for the faithlessness of their fathers. Why forty years? One year for each day their fathers spent murmuring in the wilderness (verse 34).

Verses 36-38 explain the deaths of the spies who were sent out (see chapter 13) and who advised against going into Canaan. Again, Caleb and Joshua are excepted.

The Results of the Attack (14:39-45)

These verses narrate an ill-fated attempt to enter Canaan from the south. In verse 39, Moses communicates God's decision to the people. They *mourned*, but decide to try it anyway (*we will go up to the place which the* LORD *has promised*). Moses advises against this idea, stating that the Lord will not be with them. This means the ark of the covenant will not accompany them into battle (see verse 44).

Against Moses' advice the people go up to the hill country, without Moses and without the ark. The Amalekites (verse 45) were nomadic people known for their ferocity in battle. The Canaanites were people who were already settled in the area. These two groups defeated the Israelites and chased them as far as Hormah, which is near Beersheba, in the southern part of Canaan.

Cereal and Drink Offerings (15:1-16)

This section interrupts the narrative of wilderness wanderings to explain some rituals and regulations concerning cereal and drink offerings to God. These verses expand on the legislation in Leviticus 2 by further explaining the cereal and drink offerings that must be made along with burnt or peace offerings. According to these verses, the amounts of offerings relate to what kind of animal is sacrificed. A sheep requires the smallest amount of offering to accompany it, then the ram, and then the bull.

A pleasing odor (NRSV) or *aroma pleasing* (NIV) (verses 3, 10, 13) symbolizes an offering that is acceptable to God.

Cereal offerings were made of uncooked flour with oil mixed into it. *A tenth of an ephah* amounts to about a tenth of a bushel; *a fourth* (NRSV) or *quarter* (NIV) *of a hin* equals a little more than one quart, since a hin was about eleven pints, or about five and one-half quarts.

The repetitive language in this section is reminiscent of the language of Numbers 1, indicating that the same writer is at work in this present section.

Verses 13-16 make the point that the sojourners who were present among the Israelites were subject to the same rules and regulations as were the Israelites themselves. The frequent references to sojourners in the historical narratives indicate that there were a significant number of these persons in Israelite society at that time.

Offering of the First Fruits (15:17-21)

The laws concerning the offering of the *first fruits* are also discussed in Leviticus 23:9-14. The offering is made of coarse meal, a substance that evidently could be made into cakes that were then baked.

Laws Concerning Atonement (15:22-31)

This section expands on the laws in Leviticus 4 concerning the sin offering. The sins under consideration in this section are mainly those that are performed unintentionally.

The statement in verse 23 (onward throughout your generations) indicates that the law is constantly evolving after the initial provision of the Ten Commandments.

According to these verses, there are two kinds of unintentional sin: sin by the community (covered in verses 24-26) and sin by an individual (covered in verses 27-28). In these regulations, the focus is on the offering itself, not on the ritual which was to accompany the offerings, as in Leviticus 4.

Sins that were committed *high-handedly* (NRSV) or *defiantly* (NIV) (verse 30) were done intentionally. According to this section, no offering can make up for this kind of sin. The person who commits this kind of sin will be *cut off,* that is, stoned to death.

Penalty for Violating the Sabbath (15:32-36)

According to these verses, the penalty for violating the sabbath is death (see also Exodus 31:14-15). The writer uses an example of a man gathering sticks. Until Moses and Aaron could decide on what the law demanded, the man was put into custody. The answer was given by divine oracle: The man was to be put to death. According to Exodus 35:3, lighting a fire on the sabbath was prohibited; perhaps this law assumes that gathering sticks was for no other purpose than lighting a fire.

The Israelites Are to Wear Tassels (15:37-41)

God commands Moses to, in turn, command the people to make tassels and wear them *on the corners of their garments*. These corners referred to the four corners on a piece of cloth that was used to make a cloak (see Deuteronomy 22:12). The purpose of this regulation was so that the people would be constantly reminded of God, God's presence, and God's commandments.

Korah and Others Revolt (16:1-15)

This section narrates a rebellion against Moses and Aaron, led by four men from the tribes of Levi and Reuben. When all involved were assembled, the total number of persons involved was 250.

According to verse 3, the complaint against Moses and Aaron was that they thought themselves to be more holy than others in the congregation. Verses 4-7 contain Moses' first response to the challenge against him. Moses suggests that a sign from God is needed to settle the matter. This sign will indicate who is authorized to approach the altar (*come near to* (NIV) or *approach* (NRSV) God).

Korah and his men are to put fire in censers (metal vessels used to handle hot coals). That is, they are to prepare an incense offering to God. In Leviticus 10:1-3, Nadab and Abihu, sons of Aaron, were struck down for offering an unholy fire in this same fashion.

Moses' second response is found in verses 8-11. These verses may be a later addition, since the second introduction in verse 8 breaks the flow of the narrative.

Here Moses accuses Korah and his companions of the same thing they accused Moses and Aaron of earlier—exalting themselves over others. Korah and the other *Levites* are not satisfied with the special status among the people. They want to be part of the *priesthood*. Moses replies that the priesthood belongs to Aaron; it was given to him by God.

Verses 12-15 describe an incident in which Dathan and Abiram, who were part of the earlier revolt (see verse 1), refuse to answer a summons by Moses. They accuse Moses of (1) not delivering on the promise of the Promised Land, and (2) wanting to *lord it over* everyone else. Dathan and Abiram are Reubenites who are not mentioned anywhere else in the Old Testament. In verse 16, Moses becomes angry and objects to the complaints lodged against him.

Korah and Others Are Punished (16:16-35)

This section expands on the instruction Moses gave earlier (see verses 5-7). Verse 18 paints a picture of 250 men, each holding a burning censer, standing at the door of the tent of meeting. There the *glory of the LORD appeared* (verse 19). By that time Korah had summoned the *whole congregation* (NRSV) or *assembly* (NIV)to witness the sight.

In verses 20-24, God commands Moses and Aaron to remove themselves from the group so they will not participate in the divine punishment. Moses and Aaron object, saying that the whole congregation (who by that time has assembled) is not guilty. God responds by removing the whole group except Korah, Dathan, and Abiram.

Verses 25-35 narrate the conclusion of the story about the fate of Dathan and Abiram. They and their families are summoned by Moses to come out and stand in front of their dwellings. The earth opens and swallows them up, indicating (according to Moses) God's displeasure with their rebellion against Moses. Nothing is said about the aftermath of this gruesome scene, except that the rest on the congregation flees in terror. Then, in verse 35, the story concludes with the destruction of the 250 men of Korah who were holding censers at the tent of meeting.

Appendix (16:36-50)

This section explains that the 250 men were not authorized to offer the incense offering. This attitude is curious, in light of the fact that Moses had commanded them to do just that (see verses 6-7). This section also explains the bronze covering on the altar, by saying it was made of the censers as a symbol for the lives of these men.

In verses 41-50, Moses' and Aaron's actions against the men of Korah are justified. The congregation challenges them for killing the people of the LORD. God responds by sending a plague of some kind, and then causing it to cease as suddenly as it began.

§ § § § § § §

The Message of Numbers 13–16

The events and stories narrated in this section intrigue us, and sometimes we are shocked at their contents. In order to understand their true meaning for the Israelite people at that time, we need to understand what was happening among the people during those troubled times. These stories give us some insights into the nature of Israel's God and the relationship between God and the chosen people.

§ The first report brought back by the spies argued against the taking of Canaan, the Promised Land. The story's point is that the land was promised by God. By hesitating to enter the land, the people were demonstrating their faithlessness in God.

§ Even the leadership of Moses and Aaron was sometimes not enough to support the people during this difficult time of wilderness wandering.

§ God became angry with the people on account of their lack of trust. However, when Moses interceded on their behalf, God repented of the decision to choose another people in their place.

§ God's mercy does not take the place of God's judgment, however. The people are to be punished for their faithlessness.

§ According to ancient justice, a man's family was to be punished for his sin. Also, the early Israelites believed that all circumstances were attributable directly to God, as punishment for disobedience. So, although we may be shocked at the fate of the families of Dathan and Abiram, in Israelite thought their fate was easily explained.

§ § § § § § §

PART SIX

Numbers 17–21

Introduction to These Chapters

These five chapters contain a variety of material, including information about the Levites, legislation concerning contact with the dead, and further narratives about the wilderness journey.

Chapters 17–21 may be outlined as follows.
I. Aaron's Rod Blossoms (17:1-13)
II. Duties of the Priests and Levites (18:1-32)
    A. The Aaronites and Levites are different (18:1-7)
    B. Portions for the priests and Levites (18:8-32)
III. Laws of Purification (19:1-22)
    A. The ritual of the red heifer (19:1-10)
    B. The water is used for cleansing (19:11-22)
IV. The Israelites Leave Kadesh (20:1-29)
    A. Water flows from rock (20:1-13)
    B. Passage through Edom (20:14-21)
    C. The death of Aaron (20:22-29)
V. The Itinerary (21:1-13)
VI. Israel Defeats the Amorites (21:14-35)

Aaron's Rod Blossoms (17:1-13)

This section narrates an incident that the writer intends to illustrate the special status of Aaron (and the tribe of Levi, of which he is the head) among the rest of the congregation. This incident is designed to put an end to all the rebellions against Moses and Aaron.

Ancestral tribes (NIV) or *houses* (NRSV)(verse 2) refers

to a tribe, since the total number of rods is twelve, one for each tribe. The rods used in this demonstration are probably sticks with no protruding branches on them. According to the command of God, each of these rods has the name of one of the tribal leaders on it.

According to verses 6-7, Moses carries out God's instructions to the letter. As a result, Aaron's rod blossoms and produces almonds, signifying Aaron's special place as a leader of the people. Therefore, the people are not to murmur against him any more. Aaron's rod is to be kept in front of the ark from now on, as a reminder of his special status and authority.

The Aaronites and Levites Are Different (18:1-7)

This section intends to draw the distinction between the Aaronites and the Levites. The Aaronites are the sons of Aaron, and the Levites are *your ancestral house* (NRSV) or *your father's family* (NIV), that is, the rest of the tribe of Levi, of which Aaron and his sons are a special part. They are set aside for special duties related to the tabernacle.

Whereas the Aaronites are to attend to the duties of the altar and sanctuary, the Levites are to minister to the Aaronites and attend to other duties related to the tabernacle. They are not to touch the holy vessels inside the tabernacle; this responsibility is given to the Aaronites, since they are given the *priesthood* (verse 7). This entire section is actually an answer to the question raised by the people earlier (see 17:13). The Aaronites are the ones designated to come near to the tabernacle.

Portions for the Priests and Levites (18:8-32)

The *portion* refers to a certain percentage of offerings brought by the congregation. This portion goes to the priests (Aaron and his sons) and the rest of the Levites, since the duties of these persons precludes them from growing their own food.

The most holy things belong only to Aaron and his sons, the priests. Verses 9-10 describe what these holy things are: cereal offerings, sin offerings, and guilt offerings. Leviticus 1–7 describes these offerings in more detail. They are to be eaten by the priests in a most holy place (that is, inside the tabernacle).

Verses 11-18 list other offerings the priests and their families may eat: oil, wine, grain, first fruits, and devoted things (the firstborn of animals). The *wave* (NIV) or *elevation* (NRSV) *offering* (verse 11) refers to the manner in which the offering is presented at the altar—it is waved back and forth when it is offered.

Redemption (verses 15-17) refers to payment of money that substitutes for the firstborn of humans and unclean animals, which, of course, cannot be sacrificed.

A *covenant of salt* (verse 19) refers to food seasoned with salt and eaten at a special meal at which a covenant is made. Verse 20 concludes the section by summarizing the special status of the Aaronites, as ordained by God.

With verse 21 the writer turns his attention to the Levites, who are to receive the Israelites' tithe as their special portion. The rest of verses 21-24 repeats what was already said about the Levites in verses 1-7. The *tithe* is a tax amounting to ten percent of the produce from the land.

According to verses 25-32, the Levites are to take the tithe and divide it—nine-tenths goes to them and one-tenth goes to the Aaronites (*a tithe of the tithe* (NRSV) or *a tenth of a tithe* (NIV).

The Ritual of the Red Heifer (19:1-10)

These verses contain instructions given to Moses and Aaron concerning the ceremony of purification. The people are to bring a *red heifer* (young cow) that is (1) unblemished, and (2) has never been used for plowing. Why the animal needs to be red is not stated.

This heifer is to be slaughtered in the presence of a

priest (here Eleazar), who then sprinkles her blood toward the front of the tabernacle. He is to do this *seven times*, since seven is a sacred number. The animal is then burned in the presence of the priest (verse 5). The priest adds several ingredients to the fire (see also Leviticus 14:4); these items have a purifying effect.

According to verses 7-8, the priest, who is unclean due to his contact with the dead animal, and the person who burned the animal, are both *unclean until evening*. Someone who is clean then gathers the ashes and places them outside the camp to be used later in the *water for cleansing* (removal of sin). That person also becomes unclean until the evening (verse 10).

The Water Is Used for Cleansing (19:11-22)

This section describes how one can become clean by purification, after becoming unclean by contact with a dead body (see Leviticus 21:1-12).

The water (verse 12) is the water of purification mentioned earlier in verse 9.

Whoever does not go through the cleansing ritual on the third and seventh days will be *cut off* (verse 13), that is, put to death. That person defiles not only himself, but the tabernacle as well.

Verses 14-19 deal with specific instances of uncleanness due to contact with the dead. First, if someone dies inside a tent, the persons and objects become unclean. Second, in an open field a dead body must be actually touched in order to make a person unclean.

Verses 17-18 discuss how these circumstances of uncleanness are to be remedied. *Ashes* (verse 17) are the ashes of the heifer mentioned in verse 9. *Running water* (NRSV) refers to *fresh water* (NIV) that comes from a spring or a brook. *Hyssop* is a bushy shrub.

Verses 20-22 elaborate on the information provided earlier, in verse 13.

Water Flows from Rock (20:1-13)

These verses narrate an incident in which God
provides water as a sign for the thirsty people. This
episode is parallel to the story narrated in Exodus 17:1-7.
Here the story provides the reason that the Israelites
were not allowed to enter the Promised Land.

Verse 1 introduces the story and sets the scene. The
Israelites need to detour on the east side of the Jordan
River, after an unsuccessful attempt to enter Canaan
from the southwest (see chapters 13–14). They have been
at Kadesh for quite some time (see 13:26), and are now
ready to make a move.

Our brothers (NIV) or *kindred* (NRSV) (verse 3) refers to
Dathan and Abiram (see chapter 15).

Moses and Aaron take the people's (by now familiar)
complaints to God at the door of the tabernacle.
According to verse 12, God accuses Moses of unbelief,
and his punishment is that he is not allowed to enter the
Promised Land. In this story, we see no evidence of
Moses' unbelief, however.

Verse 13 is a summary statement explaining why this
area is called *Meribah*, to symbolize the *contention*
between God and the people that was evident in this
incident.

Passage Through Edom (20:14-21)

These verses form a transition between the wilderness
wanderings and the conquest of the Promised Land.
Obviously, from Kadesh the most sensible route into
Canaan would have been through Edom. Therefore, the
people request passage through that territory. *Your
brother* (verse 14) refers to Edom as the brother of Israel,
or Jacob (see Genesis 25:24-26). The Edomites were
descendants of Esau.

Despite a long explanation of what the Israelites have
endured in recent years, the king of Edom is
unimpressed (see verses 19-21).

The *King's Highway* (verse 17) refers to a north-south route through the heart of Edomite territory. This trade route would have been large enough to accommodate the wagons that would have accompanied the king's entourage.

The Death of Aaron (20:22-29)
The incident of Aaron's death takes place at Mount Hor, which is located on the border of Edomite territory. This story serves as a reminder of why the Israelites will not enter the Promised Land (see also 20:12).

According to this account, Aaron's leadership passes to his elder son, Eleazar. The garments that are transferred are those commonly worn by the priests (see Exodus 28). This entire incident is reminiscent of the story of the death of Moses (see Deuteronomy 34).

The Itinerary (21:1-13)
Verses 1-3 describe a battle that took place at the city of Hormah (see also Numbers 14:39-45). This account explains the derivation of the name *Hormah* (the name means *utter destruction*). Hormah was located about ten miles east of Beersheba.

This section is probably a later insertion into the narrative of the Israelite conquest of Canaan, since Hormah is not located near the territory of Edom (where the Israelites were located at the time). Why this incident is recorded here is difficult to determine. The name *Hormah* is explained in another way in Judges 1:17.

From Mount Hor the Israelites journey southward toward the Gulf of Aqabah and the city of Ezion-geber. No one knows for certain the derivation of the name *Atharim* (verse 1).

Verses 4-9 narrate Moses' making of the bronze serpent. Here the people resort again to complaining about their fate in the wilderness, and the result is punishment. They are bitten by fiery serpents. After the people confess their sin, Moses intercedes on their behalf and God relents and offers a way out.

The *bronze snake* (NIV) or *serpent of bronze* (NRSV) is a cultic object worshiped by the Canaanites; it is called *Nehushtan* in 2 Kings 18:4. The fact that this object is called by several different names in this passage may indicate a combination of different sources.

According to verses 10-13, the Israelites go northward through the region east of the Jordan River. Their detour around Edom is finished. They are now in eastern Moab. *Arnon* (verse 13) is on the northern border of Moab. *Toward the sunrise* means to the east.

Israel Defeats the Amorites (21:14-35)

This section describes a war between Israel and Sihon, the king of the Amorites. The *Book of the Wars of the Lord* (verse 14) refers to a collection of poetry that is no longer available to us. This section also explains the derivation of the Arnon, and its location near Moab.

Verse 16 explains the name *Beer* (the name means *well*). Apparently there must have been a well at that location. This explanation in turn causes a quotation of an ancient poem about digging a well.

Verses 18-20 contain a list of places whose locations are now unknown.

Verses 21-30 describe the battle. The Amorites lived just north of Moab. They were defeated by the Israelites in this battle.

The request in verse 21 is similar to the earlier request made by the Israelites to pass through the territory of Edom (see 20:14-16). Here, however, the Israelites do not back down when the king refuses to allow them passage.

Verses 25-26 introduce the song that is contained in verses 27-30. The song focuses on Heshbon, which is the residence of Sihon, king of the Amorites. The grammar and the vocabulary of this song are ancient, and therefore difficult to understand and interpret. The song is a taunt song, which carries the message that King Sihon had already captured Moab in an earlier battle, including the city of Heshbon. Otherwise, the existence of Heshbon in Amorite territory would be difficult to understand.

Chemosh (verse 29) is the national god of Moab.

According to verses 33-35, the battle with the people of Bashan resulted in victory for the Israelites. Bashan was located just north of the Jabbok River, east of the river Jordan.

§ § § § § § §

The Message of Numbers 17–21

§ God sometimes designates an individual or individuals, such as Moses and Aaron, and provides them with special skills to support them in positions of authority over others.

§ The office of the priesthood involves special responsibilities that include bearing the burden of the sins and mistakes of others within the congregation.

§ Unbelief is not tolerated among the people of God. Unbelief can cause punishment, although God can repent of that decision if persuaded that the people will change their ways.

§ § § § § § §

PART SEVEN Numbers 22–24

Introduction to These Chapters

These three chapters include the story of Balaam and Balak, as well as four oracles delivered by Balaam the seer. The story takes place in the plains of Moab, while the Israelites were making preparations to enter that territory.

Here is an outline of Numbers 22–24.
I. Balak Summons Balaam the Seer (22:1-40)
   A. Balak sends for Balaam twice (22:1-20)
   B. Balaam's talking donkey (22:21-40)
II. Four Oracles of Balaam (22:41–24:25)
   A. Introduction and first oracle (22:41–23:10)
   B. Introduction and second oracle (23:11-24)
   C. Introduction and third oracle (23:25–24:9)
   D. Introduction and fourth oracle (24:10-25)

Balak Sends for Balaam Twice (22:1-20)

The plains of Moab (verse 1) are located in the region across the Jordan at Jericho. Across the Jordan means the western side of that river, assuming a starting point north and east of the northern end of the Dead Sea. Crossing over the Jordan meant crossing from east to west, since the Israelites moved into Canaan on the eastern side of the Dead Sea.

Balak is the king of Moab at the time. He evidently has heard of the defeat of the Amorites (see 21:21-35), and he and his people are afraid of these powerful Israelites. The word *Moab* in verse 4 designates the king of Moab, who acts and speaks on behalf of all the people. The people of Moab have an alliance with the Midianites, so it is natural to approach the elders of that territory for help in dealing with the Israelites. What response comes from the Midianites is not indicated in the text; they are not mentioned again in this story.

According to verses 5-6, Balak sends messengers to Balaam, a seer who lives in the *land of Amaw* (NRSV) or as translated by the NIV *in his native land* near the River (meaning the Euphrates River, in Mesopotamia). These messengers request, on Balak's behalf, that Balaam come back with them to curse the Israelites so they will not encircle the Moabites and defeat them.

It is interesting that Balaam, a Mesopotamian diviner, would consider himself subject to the will of Israel's God. When Balak hears Balaam's response he is not discouraged. He sends more messengers with more money. This time God agrees that Balaam can return with the messengers to Moab, but can only act and speak at the command of God.

Balaam's Talking Donkey (22:21-40)

According to verse 22, Balaam sets out for Moab but is stopped along the way and confronted by an *angel* (messenger) of God. Apparently, God has become angry with Balaam because he is headed for Moab. This response is curious in light of God's earlier instructions in 22:20; perhaps this is an older story that was inserted here with the rest of the Balaam material.

This whole narrative is a good example of Israelite storytelling and humor. Its message is that sometimes even an animal can see things that human beings, in their stubbornness, cannot understand. The speaking donkey is reminiscent of the talking serpent Eve encounters in Genesis 3.

As we read this story we wonder about the response of

the Moabite messengers that were traveling with Balaam. The narrator does not tell us where they were located or what they thought about these strange circumstances. Verses 34-35 conclude the narrative by describing Balaam's recognition that he is speaking and acting only what God intends. The readers are thus reminded of that fact as well.

In verses 36-40, Balaam and Balak finally meet at the northern border of Moab. This location signifies that Balak respects Balaam to the extent that he is willing to travel to the limits of his territory to meet him. At the same time, however, Balak is perturbed that it took Balaam so long to get there.

Kiriath-huzoth cannot be located with certainty. The sacrifices that take place there bring Balaam symbolically into the community of Balak.

Introduction and First Oracle (22:41–23:10)

This section begins a series of four subsections, each containing a prose introduction followed by an oracle in poetic form. These oracles are delivered at a place called *Bamoth-baal* (which means *high places of Baal*). This hill is evidently high enough so that Balaam can easily see those he is to curse. (Balak still thinks that Balaam has come to curse the Israelites.)

Balak prepares a sacrifice according to Balaam's instructions. Balaam then goes to an adjacent hill to receive a word from God. The message God gives the Moabites (through Balaam) follows in verses 7-10. The content of this oracle generally repeats what was narrated in the earlier story.

Aram (verse 7) refers to Mesopotamia. The *eastern mountains* are mountains in the Arabian desert, in the region of Mesopotamia.

According to verse 9, Israel does not consider itself one of the nations. In other words, Israel is different from other nations, presumably on account of its God.

Verse 10 refers to the large number of the Israelites, a fact that had earlier terrified the Moabites. Balaam prays that his refusal to curse Israel will allow him to die the death of a righteous man.

Introduction and Second Oracle (23:11-24)

This second oracle is introduced by verses 11-17, which narrate a repetition of the sequence of events in 23:1-6. Balak is angry, and decides to try viewing the Israelites from another hill. According to Balak, perhaps a different view will change Balaam's (and God's) mind.

The *field of Zophim* (verse 14) means *field of the spies*. It is located on top of Mount Pisgah, somewhere in the southern end of the Jordan valley, on the east side of the river. Its exact location is unknown.

Balak makes the same preparations for sacrifice this time as he did previously (see 23:1-6).

The oracle proper appears in verses 18-24. Balaam addresses Balak, defending God's character. Unlike human beings, God is constant and unchangeable.

Shout of a king (NIV) or *acclaimed as a king* (NRSV) (verse 21) refers to the noise that accompanies the arrival of a king in the midst of his people. *Horns of the wild ox* (NRSV)(verse 22) symbolizes God's awesome power *as strong as a wild ox* (NIV). In general, Balaam's message is a blessing on the Israelites, not a curse.

Introduction and Third Oracle (23:25–24:9)

The third oracle (in 24:3-9) is introduced in 23:25–24:2. Balak becomes exasperated because things are not going his way, and he commands Balaam to say nothing at all. Apparently, he realizes that Balaam has no intention of cursing these Israelites.

Verses 27-30 repeat 23:13-14 word for word. The only exception is the location of the move—here Balaam and Balak move to the top of Mount Peor and make the same preparations for a sacrifice. Mount Peor is in the same general location as Mount Pisgah.

Balaam is introduced as a man whose eye is clear (see verse 3). This description probably reflects the fact that Balaam is a seer. Israel is described in this oracle as a prosperous and secure nation.

Agag (verse 7) may refer to the Amalekite king who reigned during the rule of Saul, in about 1100 B.C. (see 1 Samuel 15:8).

Introduction and Fourth Oracle (24:10-25)

The introduction to the fourth oracle of Balaam is found in verses 10-14; the oracle proper is in verses 15-24. Balak becomes angry again, and strikes his hands together (verse 10). He then reproaches Balaam again (verse 11). Balaam responds by repeating what he had said earlier (see 22:18). Then he delivers his fourth oracle without the usual preparations beforehand.

This fourth oracle is different from the others because it is future-oriented (see verses 17-19). Its message is that Israel will defeat Moab and Edom, led by a *star* and a *scepter* (symbols for kingly authority).

The sons of Sheth (NRSV) or *Shethites* (NIV) (verse 17) is a designation for the Moabites; its derivation is uncertain. *Seir* (verse 18) is another name for Edom.

According to verses 20-24, Balaam takes up several other discourses, first concerning the Amalekites (verse 20) and then concerning the Kenites (verses 21-22). The Amalekites were nomads living in the southern portion of Canaan, and the Kenites lived in the hill country of Judah.

The last of these additional discourses is found in verses 23-24. Here the text is poorly preserved and quite difficult to understand. It is addressed to no one in particular.

Verse 25 brings the entire Balaam story to its conclusion.

§ § § § § § §

The Message of Numbers 22–24

§ God can use foreigners (non-Israelites) to communicate with the chosen people and to fulfill the divine purposes.

§ Balaam is firm in his conviction (despite financial incentives) that he must do and say only what God intends. This resolve speaks to his firm faith.

§ Sometimes humans, because of their stubbornness, cannot see the obvious truth in a situation.

§ Israel is a nation chosen by God and set aside for a special relationship with God. Nothing Israel can do is sinful enough to remove that basic relationship.

§ God, unlike human beings who are subject to change, is constant and immovable.

§ § § § § § §

Numbers 25–27

Introduction to These Chapters

In this section we find further stories related to the territory of Moab, an account of a second census taken by Moses and Eleazar, and a discussion of the laws regarding inheritance of property by women. At the end of this section, Joshua is commissioned by God to take the place of Moses in the conquest of the Promised Land.

Numbers 25–27 may be outlined as follows.
I. Disobedience in Moab (25:1-18)
II. Moses Takes Another Census (26:1-65)
  A. Introduction (26:1-4)
  B. The census (26:5-51)
  C. Land allotments (26:52-56)
  D. Census of the Levites (26:57-65)
III. The Daughters of Zelophehad (27:1-11)
IV. Joshua Succeeds Moses (27:12-23)

Disobedience in Moab (25:1-18)

This rather long section concerns the relationships between Israel and other nations. Verses 1-12 narrate two incidents that take place in the territory of Moab. In the first incident (verses 1-5), the people were living in *Shittim*, near the city of Jericho. To indulge in sexual immorality (verse 1) means to participate in cultic rites with the women of Moab. Apparently the men of Israel also ate sacrifices prepared for the Moabite god, Baal of Peor, an act that was offensive to Israel's God.

According to ancient philosophy, hanging the leaders of the people atones for the sin of the whole community.

In the second incident (verses 6-9), one of the men of Israel brings a Midianite woman into the camp, presumably to marry her. The assumption was that if he married her he would also succumb to the worship of her gods. The results of this union are disastrous. The man and the woman are both killed by the priest Phinehas, and a plague destroys 24,000 Israelites.

Why Moses and the people were weeping at the door of the tent of meeting (verse 6) is not stated. Perhaps they were upset at the execution and plague mentioned previously.

Verses 10-18 describe what happens to Phinehas as a result of his actions in verse 8. He is given a *covenant of peace*, signifying his relationship with God. He is also given the office of high priest as a reward for his dedication.

Verses 14-15 provide the names of the unfortunate couple, and verses 16-18 blame the whole incident on the Midianites. The results of continuing strife between Israel and Midian will be seen later in chapter 31.

Introduction (26:1-4)

After the plague described in 25:9 it was evidently necessary to take another census to determine how strong the Israelites were militarily. The wording of God's instructions is similar to the first set of instructions given in chapter 1.

Eleazar has now taken the place of Aaron, his father, who died on Mount Hor (see 20:22-29). Now the people are located in the *Plains of Moab* on the east side of the Jordan River, opposite Jericho.

The Census (26:5-51)

Twelve tribes are listed, including Ephraim and Manasseh, the two sons of Joseph, who take the place of the Levites, who were not counted with the rest (making the total number of tribes twelve). The lists are quite similar to those given in chapter 1.

For each tribe, its clans are listed. With Reuben, a special note is included concerning the fate of Dathan and Abiram (see Numbers 16).

Simeon's numbers are much less than they were in the earlier census; perhaps this tribe occupied a location in which it was vulnerable to raids from enemy people. On the other hand, the totals for Benjamin and Manasseh are significantly higher.

Verse 51 gives the total number of Israelites as 601,730, slightly lower than the earlier census (603,550; see Numbers 1:46).

Land Allotments (26:52-56)

The census provides the basis for allotting land when it all comes under Israelite control. The guidelines given are that the tribes are to receive land allotments according to their relative size.

Census of the Levites (26:57-65)

The Levites are counted separately because they have no land allotment. They are divided into three groups as in Numbers 3: the Gershonites, the Kohathites, and the Merarites. The total number of Levites is 23,000, whereas the total of 22,000 is given in 3:39. The reason for the disparity is not stated.

Verses 63-65 conclude this section with a reminder that these Israelites now being counted are a different generation than those counted in the first census.

The Daughters of Zelophehad (27:1-11)

In this section a legal case is brought before Moses and Eleazar for a decision. Zelophehad is from the tribe of Manasseh, and he has five daughters and no sons. This circumstance presented an interesting dilemma. On the one hand, a man's inheritance was always to stay within his family (see 1 Kings 21:3, for example). On the other hand, women did not inherit property. So what will happen to Zelophehad's inheritance when he dies?

This question is evidently too difficult for Moses and Eleazar to answer, so they present the case to God for a determination (verses 5-11). The order of inheritance is given as follows: the man's sons; the man's daughters if there are no sons; the man's brothers if there are no children; the man's uncles if there are no brothers; any other male relatives if there are no uncles. It is interesting that no thought is given to a man's wife if he should die and leave her as a survivor.

This legislation is repeated in Numbers 36.

Joshua Succeeds Moses (27:12-23)

The death of Moses, implied here in verses 12-14, is described in more detail in the final chapters of the book of Deuteronomy. God instructs Moses to go up onto the *Abarim range*, which is evidently a mountain range that included Mount Nebo, the site of Moses' death. Moses is to view the Promised Land from this location, which is somewhere near the north end of the Dead Sea.

God tells Moses that he will be *gathered to your people*, meaning that he will die. Like Aaron, Moses is not allowed to enter the Promised Land because of his unbelief evidenced in the incident at Meribah (see Numbers 20:12-13).

In verses 15-17 Moses asks God to appoint a replacement to lead the people into the Promised Land. Immediately God grants Moses' request, and designates Joshua (verses 18-21). Joshua will be given God's *spirit*, just as Moses had it (see 11:17, for example).

According to God's instructions, Moses is to commission Joshua for his new task before the whole congregation. Apparently the commissioning involves passing *authority* from one man to the other. The *Urim* (verse 2) is the sacred lot the priest will use to advise Joshua in decision-making. With Joshua, the priest will facilitate communication between him and God relative to going out and coming in (that is, military maneuvers). Moses did not require this intermediary; he had a direct relationship with God.

In verses 23-25, Moses follows God's instructions immediately and to the letter.

§ § § § § § §

The Message of Numbers 25–27

§ God will not hesitate to punish the people for their apostasy (worshiping other gods). Yoking oneself to another god will bring judgment.

§ The slight decrease in the number of the Israelites during the wilderness sojourn testifies to God's presence with them and ability to sustain them despite heavy odds.

§ The law in Israel is constantly being revised according to individual circumstances. Although some basic regulations are fixed, in its detail it could be changed or reinterpreted as situations arise that are ambiguous.

§ The (impending) death of Moses does not mean the end of leadership of the people. God replaces Moses with Joshua, in order that the people not be left like sheep without a shepherd.

§ § § § § § §

Numbers 28–31

Introduction to These Chapters

Numbers 28–31 contains instructions concerning offerings, regulations related to the making of vows, especially by women, and an account of a holy war between the people of Israel and the Midianites.

Chapters 28–31 may be outlined as follows.
I. Regulations Concerning Offerings (28:1–29:40)
  A. Burnt offerings (28:1-15)
  B. Feast of Unleavened Bread (28:16-31)
  C. Other festivals (29:1-38)
II. Vows Made by Women (30:1-16)
III. The Israelites Conquer Midian (31:1-54)
  A. Report of the war (31:1-12)
  B. Ceremonial purification (31:13-24)
  C. Distribution of booty (31:25-54)

Burnt Offerings (28:1-15)

This section lists sacrifices that the community is to offer on a regular basis. A pleasing odor or aroma (verse 2) signifies an offering that is acceptable to God.

Verses 3-8 describe the regular (daily) burnt offerings to be presented in the morning and evening. (See also Exodus 29:38-42.) This offering consists of two male lambs, along with a cereal offering mixed with oil. The flour and the oil together make a kind of dough. *Beaten oil* (NRSV) drips freely from beaten olives, rather than being *pressed* (NIV) out of olives.

According to verses 9-10, an additional burnt offering is to be made on the sabbath. This offering is twice the volume of the daily offerings, but it is to be offered only once on each sabbath day.

Verses 11-15 instruct that at the beginning of each month a very large burnt offering is to be made.

Feast of Unleavened Bread (28:16-31)

These verses are almost an exact repetition of Leviticus 23:5-8. In the seventh month there are special feast days. Since the new year begins in the spring, the seventh month falls during the autumn of the year.

The feast of Unleavened Bread is also discussed in Exodus 12:1-27. According to the Exodus passage, this feast begins with the celebration of the Passover, which symbolizes the escape of the Israelites from bondage in Egypt. Passover is to be held on the fourteenth day of the first month, and the festival of Unleavened Bread begins on the next day and lasts for fourteen days. The unleavened bread symbolizes the fact that the Israelites left Egypt before their bread was allowed to rise.

Verses 16-31 discuss the feast of Weeks (see also Leviticus 23:15-21).

Other Festivals (29:1-38)

Three other kinds of festivals are described in this section: the new year's festival on the first day of the seventh month (verses 1-6), the festival on the day of atonement, or the tenth day of the seventh month (verses 7-11), and the feast of booths (verses 12-38). The people are instructed concerning what kind of offerings they are to make during these celebrations.

On the fifteenth day of the seventh month there is to be a holy convocation. No work will be done on that day. That day is to be followed by seven days of celebration and offering of sacrifices (different offerings are described for each of these seven days). These seven days are then followed by an eighth day on which there will be a *sacred assembly* (NIV) or *holy convocation* (NRSV). Again, there will be no work on that day, and appropriate sacrifices will be offered.

Note that the number of bulls to be sacrificed decreases with each day, beginning with thirteen on the first day and ending with seven on the seventh day. The significance of this numbering is unknown.

Vows Made by Women (30:1-16)

This passage has no immediate connection to what precedes or follows it, except that it occurs in the context of last-minute instructions given to Moses by God before his death.

The passage begins with a statement concerning vows and pledges—that they are binding on men no matter what the circumstances. This same regulation is discussed in Leviticus 27 and in Deuteronomy 23:21-23. The Old Testament differentiates between *vows* (involving what persons will do) and *pledges* (involving what persons will not do). Vows and pledges, in order to be legitimate, must be both spoken by someone and heard by someone.

Verses 3-15 discuss vows and pledges made by women, who were generally considered to be subordinate to men in Israelite society. However, this passage makes clear that women do have the right to make vows and pledges in the first place.

According to verses 3-5, when a young (not-yet-married) woman makes a vow it is subject to her father's approval, and he may nullify it as long as he does so on the same day it is spoken and heard.

According to verses 6-8, a married woman's vow or pledge can be nullified by her husband on the same day it is spoken and heard. But according to verse 9, a widow's vow can never be nullified (as long as it is spoken and heard).

Verses 10-15 summarize the situation of what a husband can and cannot do with regard to his wife's vows. On what basis might a husband (or father) nullify a woman's vow? The writer does not say; we must assume that it is up to the man's personal preference and judgment.

Verse 16 summarizes this chapter.

Report of the War (31:1-12)

In chapter 25 (verses 16-18) the stage was set for this battle. The Midianites were apparently responsible for what happened to Israel at Peor (a plague killed 24,000 Israelites because one man brought a Midianite woman into his camp).

In verses 1-2, God instructs Moses to take revenge on the Midianites before his death. *The LORD's vengeance* (verse 3) indicates that this battle falls under the category of holy war, where all booty that is taken is dedicated to God.

In verses 4-6, one thousand men are taken from each tribe to participate in the battle, twelve thousand men in all. Phinehas is sent along with the sanctuary vessels and the trumpets that were used to sound the alarm for battle. The ark is not mentioned; perhaps the writer takes its presence for granted.

Verse 7 describes the overwhelming victory. All the male Midianites are killed, along with their five kings and Balaam the seer. Verses 9-12 summarize the grim circumstances of the Midianites. All the women and children and the possessions are brought to Moses and Eleazar, and all their cities and encampments are burned.

Ceremonial Purification (31:13-24)

Moses becomes angry because the women and children have not already been killed. He commands his officers to kill all the male children and widows. They are to spare only the young (virgin) girls, who will be used as servants or concubines. In this way, no new generation of Midianites will be able to be produced.

According to verses 19-24, after becoming unclean through contact with the dead, the soldiers are to remain outside the camp for seven days. They are to wash themselves on the third day and on the seventh day. The procedures for this ritual washing are found in Numbers 19.

The articles mentioned in verse 20 are those that could absorb the uncleanness more readily than other items. According to verses 21-24, metal objects that might have become unclean had to be burned and cleaned with the *water for purification* (NRSV) or *cleansing* (NIV) (see Numbers 19:9). Verse 24 gives the instruction for the soldiers to return to camp after all these purification rites have been completed.

Distribution of Booty (31:25-54)

At the conclusion of any battle, the booty (possessions of the defeated people) need to be distributed fairly among the tribes. Verses 25-30 give the law for how this distribution is to take place. First, the booty is to be divided into two equal parts—one for the soldiers and one for the rest of the congregation. Then the soldiers are to pay back one portion out of 500 (one-fifth of one percent) to the priests (the *tribute for the* LORD). The rest of the congregation are to give two percent back, but their portion is to be given to the Levites, not the priests.

Verses 32-47 provide details about the booty that was distributed to the twelve tribes.

According to verses 48-54, the officers in Moses' army bring the gold and silver found among the booty to Moses and Eleazar (this precious metal was alluded to earlier, in verse 22).

§ § § § § § §

The Message of Numbers 28–31

§ Feasts, festivals, offerings, and sacrifices were all part of the ritual that had to be observed by the Israelites in order to maintain a proper relationship with God.

§ Women were considered to be of less value than men in the patriarchal society of Israel. However, once spoken and heard, a legitimate vow (whether made by a man or a woman) must be kept at all costs.

§ Worship of foreign gods was not tolerated among the Israelites.

§ § § § § § §

Numbers 32–36

Introduction to These Chapters

These chapters include a description of the land
allotment east of the Jordan River, a summary of Israel's
wilderness wanderings from the time the people left
Egypt, a description of the ideal boundary lines in the
land of Canaan, a description of the cities the Levites
were to inhabit as well as the cities of refuge, and
regulations about the inheritance of property.

Here is an outline of these chapters.
  I. The Territory of Reuben and Gad (32:1-42)
      A. Introduction and speech of Moses (32:1-15)
      B. Tribal allotments (32:16-42)
  II. The Israelites' Journey (33:1-49)
      A. Introduction (33:1-4)
      B. From Ramses to Sinai (33:5-15)
      C. From Sinai to Kadesh-barnea (33:16-36)
      D. From Kadesh-barnea to the Jordan (33:37-49)
      E. Final instructions (33:50-56)
 III. The Boundaries of the Land (34:1-29)
  IV. The Cities of Refuge (35:1-54)
      A. Cities given to the Levites (35:1-8)
      B. Cities of refuge described (35:9-15)
      C. Laws concerning killing (35:16-34)
   V. Inheritance of Property (36:1-13)

Introduction and Speech of Moses (32:1-15)

Since the Israelites have thus far conquered some of

the land east of the Jordan River, some of the tribes want to settle there rather than on the other side of the Jordan, where the land is yet unconquered. These tribes (Reuben and Gad) promise to participate in the conquest of the land west of the Jordan, and to return to their own allotted land at a later time.

Jazer and Gilead are located east of the Jordan and south of the Jabbok River. This territory was apparently good for cattle breeding, and these two tribes were well known for their large herds of cattle.

In verses 2-5 the question is posed to Moses and Eleazar. Specific cities in the area are mentioned.

According to verses 6-15, in which Moses responds to the request, his first reaction is negative. Essentially Moses' speech recapitulates the events of Numbers 13–14. The message in this chain of events is that crossing over the Jordan to inhabit the territory on the west side is part of God's plan.

Tribal Allotments (32:16-42)

Verses 16-27 narrate negotiations between Moses and the leaders of the tribes of Reuben and Gad. The result of these negotiations is a compromise. If those tribes are willing to participate in the conquest of the land on the west side of the Jordan, they may return to the east side after the conquest is over. They can build cities and inhabit them now, and their women and children will remain there until the conquest is over.

According to verses 28-33, since Moses will not live long enough to see whether the promises are fulfilled on both sides of the compromise, he sets up a group of people to follow the situation. This group of people is composed of Eleazar, Joshua, and one representative from each of the tribes.

Verses 34-38 is a list of cities built and inhabited by these tribes. All these cities are located on the east side of the Jordan River.

According to verses 39-42, some of this territory was also inhabited by the tribe of Manasseh. Machir, a son of Manasseh, apparently inhabited the area of Gilead.

Introduction (33:1-4)

This whole section intends to provide an accounting of the entire itinerary of the Israelites, from the time they left Egypt until they arrived at the Jordan River. According to verse 2, Moses wrote this itinerary down himself by the command of the LORD. Some names on this list are not found anywhere else in the Old Testament. Portions of this list could be based on another document that was available at the time this was written.

From Ramses to Sinai (33:5-15)

This section of the Israelites' itinerary is discussed in Exodus 12:37–19:2. Verse 12 mentions *Dophkah* as the next stop after the Wilderness of Sin. This location is not mentioned anywhere else in the Old Testament; nor is the site of *Alush* (verse 13).

From Sinai to Kadesh-Barnea (33:16-36)

This portion of the itinerary is found in Numbers 10:11–20:1. The places mentioned in verses 14-18*a* are found also in the earlier narrative; those mentioned in verses 18*b*-30 (*Rithmah* to *Hashmonah*) are not otherwise known.

From Kadesh-barnea to the Jordan (33:37-49)

This portion of the narrative is found in Numbers 20:22–22:1. Some of these names are known from the earlier narratives and some are not. This portion of the itinerary includes a recapitulation of the death of Aaron on Mount Hor (see verses 37-39).

Final Instructions (33:50-56)

This section contains final instructions given by God through Moses to the people as they encamp on the east side of the Jordan, ready to cross over. These instructions have to do mainly with (1) refraining from making graven images (see also Leviticus 26), and (2) a fair division of the land once the conquest is completed.

The Boundaries of the Land (34:1-29)

Verses 1-2 introduce this section and set the stage for what is to follow. Moses is to convey God's command concerning the allotment of the land west of the Jordan. First, however, this land has to be defined. This is accomplished in verses 3-12. (See also Joshua 15 and Ezekiel 47–48).

The southern boundary of the Promised Land is the Brook of Egypt (verse 5), at the northern end of the Sinai peninsula. The northern boundary is the entrance of Hamath (verse 8), which is in Syrian territory. (Actually, the Israelites did not occupy the land this far north until the time of David, about 200 years later.)

The western boundary of the Promised Land was the Mediterranean Sea, and the eastern boundary was the Jordan River, from the Sea of Galilee (here called Chinnereth) to the Dead Sea.

Verse 12 concludes this section with a summary statement.

Verses 13-29 deal with the land east of the Jordan River that was allotted to the tribes of Reuben, Gad, and Manasseh. These verses make specific the group designated earlier to follow through on the promises made on both sides of the compromise (see chapter 32).

Cities Given to the Levites (35:1-8)

Because the Levites are not given any land allotments (see Leviticus 25:32-34), they are allotted special cities instead. These cities are spread throughout the land. Each one is surrounded by a certain amount of pastureland, so the Levites can raise livestock. The levitical cities number forty-eight in all, including the six cities of refuge (see below). Each of the twelve tribes donates some of these cities, according to its relative size.

Cities of Refuge Described (35:9-15)

The six cities of refuge are discussed here (see also Deuteronomy 4:41-43). Verse 11 begins the explanation of why these cities are necessary. Anyone who kills another person unintentionally may take refuge in one of these cities. The normal laws of blood revenge then do not apply. (According to the law of blood revenge, a male kinsman of a slain person must avenge the blood of his relative by killing a member of the killer's family. See Exodus 21:12-14.)

According to this description, the cities of refuge are distributed equally between the east and west sides of the Jordan River.

A person could flee to a city of refuge after a premeditated murder and thus try to take advantage of this opportunity for shelter. To guard against this possibility, a trial would be held in the presence of the congregation to determine the person's guilt or innocence.

Laws Concerning Killing (35:16-34)

This section presents a series of hypothetical cases and the judgment for each circumstance. All these cases have to do with the distinction between (intentional) murder and (unintentional) manslaughter.

Verses 16-18 have to do with the weapons used to strike someone down. If the weapon used is iron, stone, or wood, then the crime is designated as a murder. In those cases (and with a sword), the relative of the dead person has a right to blood revenge (verses 19-21).

According to verses 22-25, involuntary manslaughter is defined as an act committed suddenly (usually in anger). In that case, the person who committed the act is taken to a city of refuge to remain there until the death of the current high priest. If he leaves this city of refuge, he may be killed by his avenger who will then not be punished.

Verse 29 summarizes the preceding section. Verses 30-34 contain additional statements concerning murder. First, it takes more than one witness to convict a person of murder. Second, the death penalty is the only option for a murderer, once he is convicted. (There will be no ransom.) The reason for this law is that blood *pollutes the land* in which God dwells, and it must be avenged before the land can become clean again.

Inheritance of Property (36:1-13)

This chapter is related to Numbers 27, where the inheritance of property by women is first mentioned. The information in this chapter expands on the ruling given in chapter 27.

The earlier ruling was yes, women can inherit the property of their fathers if there are no sons in the family. Here the additional stipulation is given that these women who inherit property must marry within their own tribes. The question is posed by the leaders of the tribe of Manasseh, of which Zelophehad is a member. (This tribe is called the tribe of Joseph in verse 5; Joseph was Manasseh's father.)

For a discussion of the jubilee year (verse 4), see Leviticus 25.

When daughters who inherit money from their fathers marry within the same tribe, the inheritance always stays within the original tribe and is not transferred from one tribe to another. However, women can evidently marry men from other tribes as long as they have not inherited any property from their fathers.

According to verse 12, the daughters of Zelophehad obey the ruling handed down concerning their marriages.

Verse 13 summarizes the book of Numbers as a whole, and concludes by reminding the readers about the location of the Israelites at this point in their history.

§ § § § § § §

The Message of Numbers 32–36

§ Tribal unity was very important for the early Israelites. Thus, the tribes who wanted to settle east of the Jordan River had to first promise that they would join the other tribes in the task at hand before going off on their own. A unified Israel was needed for the conquest of the Promised Land to take place successfully.

§ Once the Israelites entered the land of Canaan, it was important that their religious lives remained pure, and not tarnished by the cultic rituals of the Canaanites. Worship of other gods in any form was not tolerated by the God of Israel.

§ Murder is a crime that offends not only the people involved, but God as well.

§ § § § § § §

Introduction to Deuteronomy

Deuteronomy is the last of the Five Books of Moses, also called the Torah. The book of Deuteronomy concludes with the death of Moses on Mount Nebo, right before the Israelites enter the Promised Land.

The narrative in Deuteronomy picks up where the book of Numbers leaves off. The Israelites are encamped in the territory of Moab, and are waiting to cross over the Jordan River and conquer the Promised Land. Because Moses knows he will not be allowed to cross over the Jordan, he takes this opportunity to say some final words to the congregation before his death.

Deuteronomy is essentially three separate addresses by Moses (chapters 1–4, 5–28, and 29–30). The overall theme of the book is law (the name *Deuteronomy* actually means *second law*).

Moses' sermons begin with a review of the events in the lives of the Israelites since the time they left Egypt (chapters 1–4). Moses continues with a discussion of the Ten Commandments (chapters 5–6). The third portion of what Moses has to say involves how to live in a right relationship with God after the people are settled in their new land (chapters 7–30). The final four chapters in Deuteronomy describe the final days of Moses' life.

Deuteronomy (or portions of this book) was probably the *book of the law* found by King Josiah in the Temple in 621 B.C. This discovery led to vast reform of Israel's religious life (see 2 Kings 22–23).

Deuteronomy 1–3

Introduction to These Chapters

These three chapters that open the book of
Deuteronomy are essentially a historical review of the
events that have happened in the life of the Israelites
since they left Egypt. This history forms the first portion
of the series of (three) sermons Moses preaches to the
congregation before his death.

Chapters 1–3 may be outlined as follows.
  I. Part One (1:1-46)
    A. Introduction (1:1-18)
    B. From Horeb to Kadesh (1:19-46)
 II. Part Two (2:1-37)
    A. From Kadesh to the kingdom of Sihon (2:1-25)
    B. The Israelites defeat Sihon (2:26-37)
III. Part Three (3:1-29)
    A. The Israelites defeat Bashan (3:1-11)
    B. Allotment of eastern territory (3:12-22)
    C. Moses will not cross over (3:23-29)

Introduction (1:1-18)
Verse 1 forms a good introduction to the book of
Deuteronomy as a whole. Just as they were at the end of
the book of Numbers, the Israelites are encamped on the
east side of the Jordan River (in the plains of Moab).
Their journey from Horeb (Sinai) to Kadesh is detailed in
verses 19-46; according to this introduction that journey

took eleven days. The locations listed in verse 2 are stopping places along the way on the wilderness journey.

The *fortieth year* (verse 3) dates this event from the time of the Exodus out of Egypt.

According to verse 5, what Moses will say to the congregation in the next thirty chapters has essentially a single theme: the law. Moses' discussion of the law is preceded, however, by a history of what has happened to the Israelites since they left Egypt (the content of chapters 1–3). There are six main parts to this historical account.

1. God appoints judges to assist Moses (1:9-18)
2. Spies enter Canaan and report (1:19-46)
3. Israel passes through Edom (2:1-8)
4. Israel passes through Moab (2:9-25)
5. Israel defeats Sihon (2:26-37)
6. Israel defeats Og (3:1-22)

Verses 6-8 introduce this history by recapitulating God's instructions for conquering the Promised Land. Verses 9-18 reiterate the story originally told in Numbers 11 of the appointment of seventy elders to assist Moses in his leadership role. Verses 13-17 of this section compare with Exodus 18:13-27.

In the Numbers 11 account Moses had complained directly to God about his problem. In the present account, however, Moses narrates that he had complained to the people, not God. The original account may have sounded somewhat harsh, in that Moses came close to accusing God for the predicament he was in. In this account, Moses and the people work together to solve the problem.

From Horeb to Kadesh (1:19-46)

During this period in the original narrative (Numbers 13–14), Israel sent spies to examine the land of Canaan and bring back a report. The people began murmuring against Moses after hearing the report, and then attempted an abortive entry into Canaan from the south. Those details are essentially repeated in the present account.

Note that the report of the spies is told a little differently in this account than in the Numbers account (see Numbers 13:25-30). The earlier account emphasized the strength of the people who were inhabiting the land of Canaan, whereas this report merely says that Canaan is a *good land*. However, the people must have been made aware of the strength of its inhabitants, given their response in verse 28.

Verse 37 says that Moses cannot enter the Promised Land on account of the people's sins as well as his own. Vicarious punishment is a new element in the current version of the story.

From Kadesh to the Kingdom of Sihon (2:1-25)

According to verse 1, Israel turns from Kadesh toward the Red Sea. From here they will head up the eastern side of the Dead Sea around the Jordan River. This section retells events that were narrated in Numbers 20:14–21:20.

Here the king of Edom is not approached with a request to pass through his territory (as he was in Numbers 20:14-21). In this present passage, God commands that the Israelites leave the Edomites alone as they pass through their territory. The Edomites themselves apparently have nothing to say in the matter.

Verses 8b-25 correspond to Numbers 21:4-20. This time they go in the direction of the wilderness of Moab. Again God commands them not to harass the people of Moab, just as they were not to harass the people of Edom.

Verse 10 mentions the *Emim* (NRSV) or *Emites* (NIV)—part of a legendary group of peoples who were large in size compared to the average Israelite. *The Horites* (NIV) or *the Horim* (NRSV) (verse 12) were early inhabitants of the area.

According to verse 13, the Israelites cross the brook

Zered (at the southern end of the Dead Sea) and go northward from there. Verse 13 adds a chronological note to the narrative. From Kadesh-barnea (see 2:1) to the brook Zered, the journey has so far taken thirty-eight years.

Verses 16-24 recall events related to Israel's passage through Ammonite territory (this territory was later given to Lot). Verses 20-23 are a parenthesis related to this Ammonite territory and its history of possession. In this historical note, the giant people are called *Rephaim* and *Zamzummim*. The *Avvim* are Canaanites who were defeated by the *Caphtorim*, people from the island of Crete.

Verse 24 summarizes the defeat of Sihon the Amorite king. Verse 25 is a general statement about the attitude of surrounding people concerning the might of the Israelite people.

The Israelites Defeat Sihon (2:26-37)

This section expands on the brief note about the Amorites in verse 24. (See the narrative in Numbers 21:21-32.)

The *wilderness* (NRSV) or *desert* (NIV) *of Kedemoth* (verse 26) is on the eastern side of the Jordan River, near the northern portion of the Dead Sea.

At God's command, the Israelites request that Sihon, king of the Amorites, let them pass peacefully through his territory. But God made his heart defiant (the spirit of Sihon) so that the Israelites could have an opportunity to wage what was to become a successful battle against the Amorites.

The battle takes place at Jahaz, about fifteen miles north of Heshbon, the capital city of the Amorite kingdom. The defeat at Jahaz is complete.

The Israelites Defeat Bashan (3:1-11)

This section begins with the standard introduction. In the original narrative in Numbers, these verses correspond to Numbers 21:33-35.

The battle takes place at *Edrei*, which is in the southern portion of Bashan, east of the Jordan River, and south of the Sea of Galilee. In verse 2, God promises to give victory to the Israelites, just as they were successful in battle against Sihon. Verse 3 summarizes the victory.

Verses 4-11 elaborate on verse 3. Some cities are listed, although they are not all listed since we are told that sixty cities are involved in the victory.

Og was reputed to be a large man (one of the Rephaim). His bed was nine cubits long (about fourteen feet), and four cubits wide (about six feet). His *bed* may actually be his coffin.

Allotment of Eastern Territory (3:12-22)

This part of Moses' retelling of the original story corresponds to Numbers 32 (see also Joshua 13). The territory given to Reuben, Gad, and Manasseh is all east of the Jordan River. In general, this land is the territory of Bashan, Gilead, and the area south of Gilead as far as the midpoint of the Dead Sea.

Verses 18-22 summarize the compromise reached earlier whereby these tribes would participate in the conquest even though their territory (east of the Jordan) was already conquered. The unity of the twelve tribes was an important part of the conquest narratives.

Moses Will Not Cross Over (3:23-29)

This portion repeats the earlier narrative found in Numbers 27:12-13. Moses appeals to God, who has shown love for the Israelites through mighty acts of power on their behalf. God refuses to answer Moses' request to be allowed to cross the Jordan. Moses reports that he suffers on your account (for the disobedience of the people). And in essence God says, now don't ask me about this again.

In the parallel account in Numbers 20:12, Moses' own unbelief helped to cause his punishment. Any guilt on the part of Moses is left out of this present account, however. Perhaps the background of this section in Deuteronomy is a tradition favorable to the character of Moses.

Here the mountain where Moses (eventually) dies is called *Pisgah*; in the Deuteronomy 34 account it is called Nebo. Either these two stories come from two separate traditions, each with its own name for this mountain, or Pisgah was one peak in a group of mountains called Nebo.

The Message of Deuteronomy 1–3

§ The unity among the twelve tribes is a crucial factor in the success of the conquest of the Promised Land. Therefore, it is very important that all the tribes (even Reuben, Gad, and Manasseh) participate in the conquest together.

§ God fights on behalf of the chosen people through their conquest of Canaan. God is behind all these events, directing the people through the leadership of Moses.

§ God is different from the gods of surrounding nations. God's mighty deeds speak on behalf of God's ability to guide the people through these experiences.

§ At times the promise of the land flowing with milk and honey looks as though it is in jeopardy. However, God will fulfill this promise.

§ The Israelites do not always understand how this promise is to be fulfilled. However, their lack of understanding should not result in a lack of faith. All events are proceeding at the will and direction of their God.

§ § § § § § §

PART TWELVE Deuteronomy 4–7

Introduction to These Chapters

These four chapters in Deuteronomy are crucial in the history of the chosen people. The section begins with the conclusion to Moses' first speech that began in chapter 1. Next comes a long description of the nature of God and why God demands obedience from the chosen people. This exhortation is followed by the Ten Commandments, which form the heart of Israelite law and faith.

Chapters 4–7 may be outlined as follows.
 I. Conclusion to Moses' First Address (4:1-40)
   A. Moses appeals for obedience (4:1-14)
   B. The character of God (4:15-40)
   C. Cities of refuge (4:41-43)
 II. Moses' Second Address (4:44–26:19)
   A. Introduction (4:44-49)
   B. The Ten Commandments (5:1-33)
   C. Moses explains the first commandment (6:1-25)
   D. Keeping the commandments (7:1-26)

Moses Appeals for Obedience (4:1-14)

Here Moses ends his recapitulation of the events in the wilderness, and turns to exhortation. His appeal for obedience is a request for a faithful response to what God has done on the people's behalf.

Verse 3 recalls the incident at Baal-peor (see Numbers 25:1-9). Moses reminds the people that those who were obedient at that time are still alive; those who were not obedient have perished.

The general message of this section is that the prerequisite for a successful life in the land of Canaan is obedience to God's commandments. Other nations will surely see Israel's success and be drawn to its God.

Verses 9-14 recall God's revelation at Sinai (here called *Horeb*). See Exodus 20:2-17. Verse 11 mentions a mountain blazing with fire, a detail not mentioned in the earlier Exodus account.

These verses emphasize that God was heard but not seen in the Sinai experience. God had *no form*. This statement is a warning against idolatry, or worship of gods that can be seen in forms or images.

The Character of God (4:15-40)

Verses 15-18 elaborate on verse 12—they are a continuation of the warning against idol worship. The idea of the one true God who cannot be represented by any image is very important to the writer of the book of Deuteronomy, and to the religious history of Israel.

Verses 16-18 list the various images that could be made but are strictly prohibited. Verse 19 states that the stars in the heavens, having been created by God in the first place, cannot be worshiped as gods, as other nations do.

Verse 20 supplies a historical note about the Exodus from Egypt. The writer's point is that the same God who brought the people out of Egypt is still with them today.

In verses 21-22, Moses reminds the people that because of *their* disobedience God will not allow him to cross the Jordan into the Promised Land. Therefore, this is his last chance to speak with them about how they should live after the conquest is over.

According to verses 25-40, the nature of God demands that the people worship no other gods—just God alone. What is the nature of God, according to this writer?

God is jealous. God demands single-minded loyalty from the chosen people.

God is merciful. God will not forsake the covenant made with the chosen people.

God is a God of history. God has accomplished great things on Israel's behalf.

God is the only God. There are no other gods in heaven or on earth.

Cities of Refuge (4:41-43)

This section is elaborated on in Deuteronomy 19. The cities of refuge were also mentioned earlier in Numbers 35. Moses had not yet named these cities, so he does so at this time. However, only half of them are designated here (those in the territory on the east side of the Jordan River). Each of the three tribes living in that territory receives a city of refuge within its boundaries.

Introduction (4:44-49)

The opening words to this section indicate that it is an introduction to what follows. The concept introduced is the law, which includes *decrees, statutes, and ordinances* (NRSV) or in the NIV: the *stipulations, decrees, and laws.* All these elements of the Law are given to the people through Moses, the intermediary.

Verses 46-49 describe briefly how the Israelites arrived at this place at this time.

The Ten Commandments (5:1-33)

Verse 1 contains a new introduction. The words *Hear, O Israel* are found frequently in the book of Deuteronomy, as Moses exhorts the people to listen to his words of advice.

Verse 2 calls the Sinai experience a *covenant* between God and the chosen people. Moses points out that he has been serving as a mediator between God and the people.

Verses 6-21 contain the Ten Commandments, with an introduction in verse 6. The first half of the commandments are explained; the second half are brief and to the point.

This account is very similar to the first account of the Ten Commandments, found in Exodus 20:2-17.

In verse 6, the words *I am the* LORD *your God* introduce the speaker as the same God who brought the people out of Egypt some years earlier. In general, the commandments are related both to God (the first five) and to other human beings (the last five).

Verse 7 is the first commandment, against having other gods. This is the most important commandment, and is thus first among the ten. The commandment assumes that there are other gods for other nations, but that there is only one God for the nation of Israel.

Verses 8-10 contain the second commandment, which is related to the first. This same subject (making graven images) is addressed in Deuteronomy 4:15-18. The third commandment (found in verse 11) protects God's name. God's name cannot be used for evil purposes (such as magic or divination).

Verses 12-15 concern observation of the sabbath, and include a lengthy explanation. But the explanation does not give the reason the sabbath is holy; rather, it explains exactly who cannot work on that day. No cultic ritual is specified for the sabbath day.

In the Exodus version of the Decalogue, the observation of the sabbath day is related to God's creation of the earth. Since God created the earth in six days and rested on the seventh, God's chosen people should also rest on the seventh day (see Exodus 20:11). In the present passage, resting on the seventh day is related to the psychological need human beings have for rest.

The commandment concerning honoring one's father and mother is based on the idea of an extended family—a concept that was prevailing in early Israelite society. In the extended family, contact with one's parents continued well beyond the teen years, unlike the situation in the nuclear family of today's American society. Note that this commandment has a positive rather than a negative orientation. The addition to this commandment is not an explanation; it is a promise.

Verse 17 refers to antisocial killing, not just any kind of killing.

The commandment in verse 18 prohibits adultery. According to Israelite custom, a man could have intercourse with his household slaves and be within the law. On the other hand, any other sexual relationships outside of marriage were prohibited by the commandment in verse 18.

The commandment against stealing (verse 19) originally prohibited specifically the stealing of persons, not property.

Verse 20 prohibits false witness against one's neighbor. The testimony of witnesses was very important in early Israelite society, since witnesses were required to convict a person of crimes such as murder.

In verse 21, the verb translated *covet* means both to covet and to take.

Verses 22-33 contain concluding statements related to the Ten Commandments. First, the point is restated that Moses served as a mediator between God and the people when the Ten Commandments were received. The people were quite willing for Moses to intercede on their behalf, because they thought that no one could see the face of God and live (see Exodus 33:20).

The second point these verses make is that Moses was the one designated to interpret the law for the people as well as to report on what the law says (verse 31).

Moses Explains the First Commandment (6:1-25)

Verses 1-3 introduce this section. *The commands* (NIV) or commandment (NRSV) (verse 1) refers to the first commandment in the decalogue, which is also the most important commandment. The statutes and ordinances will be discussed subsequently; this present section is an elaboration on the first commandment.

Note the phrase *Hear, O Israel* (verses 4 and 5). This introductory formula indicates that Moses is delivering this information in an oral form.

The promise given in verse 3 is a common one in the Book of Deuteronomy: If the people will obey the commandments, they will have a full life in the land of Canaan.

Verses 4-9 are called the *Shema* in the Hebrew tradition, based on the Hebrew word for *hear*. Since this sentence is really a noun clause, it may be translated in a variety of ways. For example, it could read *The LORD our God is one Lord*, or it could read *The LORD our God, the LORD is one*. Other translations are also possible. However the phrase is translated, the message is essentially the same.

Verse 5 expands on verse 4, stating that this God requires ultimate loyalty. In the New Testament, Jesus restates and reinterprets this commandment (see Mark 12:29-30).

These words (NRSV) (verse 6) refer to the *commandment* (NIV). Upon *your heart* means *with you always*. The people are to make certain the commandment will always be there by placing it on their hands, their foreheads, their doorposts, and their gates.

Verses 10-19 warn against complacency when the Israelites become settled in their new land. Especially because they will have many things that they did not work for (such as clothing and shelter), they will need to be careful lest they forget who gave them these things.

Fear the LORD your God (verse 13) means to be in awe of God and to be obedient. God's jealousy refers to the fact that God will not tolerate the worship of any other gods.

Put the LORD your God to the test (verse 16) means to put conditions on whether or not God will be worshiped. This kind of defiance will not be tolerated, just as it was not tolerated in the events at Massah (see Exodus 17:1-7).

In verses 20-25, a question from son to father provided the occasion to recite the creed of salvation history, beginning with Egypt and ending in the Promised Land. It is interesting that this chain of events does not include the giving of the law at Sinai; perhaps this event, because it was so central to the faith, was assumed to be included in every recitation of history.

Righteousness (NIV) or to *be in the right* (NRSV) (verse 25) means a right relationship with God.

Keeping the Commandments (7:1-26)

Verses 1-11 discuss how the Israelites are to relate to the inhabitants of Canaan once they enter that land and begin to settle there. This section reflects the anxiety (expressed often in the book of Deuteronomy) that Canaanite culture and religion will find their way into Israelite faith, bringing their corrupting influences with them.

Relationships with seven specific groups of people are banned in verse 1. The Israelites are to utterly *destroy* these people if they encounter them; that is, the booty from these battles is to be devoted to God.

In verse 5 *Asherah poles* (NIV; NRSV = *sacred poles*) were used in worship of the female goddess Asherah, a Canaanite deity.

Verse 6 explains why the Israelites are to be separate from the Canaanites: The people of Israel are *a people holy to the* LORD. Why? Because God chose them. Why did God choose them? Not because they were many in number, but because God loved them from the beginning.

Verses 12-16 conclude the sermon begun in verse 1. If the people obey the commandment, God will respond by making them plentiful.

Verses 17-26 change the subject back to the relationships between the Israelites and the other nations they will encounter in Canaan. The main point of this section comes in verse 21: Israel is not to fear these other nations. The people are to understand that when they go out to wage war against these people, God will be with them.

§ § § § § § §

The Message of Deuteronomy 4–7

§ Obedience to the commandments is a very important prerequisite for a successful life in the Promised Land.

§ Just as God remained with the people throughout their long wilderness journey, God will remain with them as they enter this next phase of their history.

§ The worship of idols in any form is not tolerated by the God of Israel. This issue is especially important because the people are about to enter Canaan with its corrupting influences.

§ The laws by which Israel was to live included regulations about relationships between people and people, as well as between people and God.

§ In every situation in which the people found themselves, they were to do their best to determine the will of God, and to do it.

§ The covenant made earlier with the patriarchs still holds true for the Israelites, and will continue to determine the actions of God on their behalf.

§ § § § § § §

Deuteronomy 8–11

Introduction to These Chapters

These chapters are concerned with how the Israelites are to live in their new land, and how they are to remain in relationship with God when their circumstances change. This material is in the form of a sermon; it continues the address Moses is giving to the people of Israel before he dies and they cross the Jordan into the Promised Land.

Here is an outline of Deuteronomy 8–11.
  I. Moses Warns Against Pride (8:1-20)
      A. God's actions in the past (8:1-10)
      B. Future prosperity (8:11-20)
 II. God's Attitude Toward Israel (9:1–10:11)
      A. God's presence with Israel (9:1-5)
      B. God's presence in history (9:6–10:11)
III. God's Requirements (10:12–11:32)
      A. God demands faithfulness and obedience (10:12-22)
      B. God wants loyalty to the covenant (11:1-25)
      C. A blessing and a curse (11:26-32)

God's Actions in the Past (8:1-10)

Here Moses seems to be repeating himself, or at least saying the same thing he has said previously, but in a slightly different way. Again, Moses reminds the people of God's care for them in the wilderness. According to

Moses, the people had to endure the wilderness experience so God could test their steadfastness.

The provision of the *manna* (verse 3) is narrated in Exodus 16 and Numbers 11. Here in this account, the manna is provided not because the people are hungry but because God wanted to teach them a lesson—that human beings cannot live by bread alone.

Verses 7-10 look to the future and describe the wealth of the land of Canaan.

Future Prosperity (8:11-20)

This section continues the thought begun in verse 7. Canaan will be a land of blessing for the Israelites. Moses exhorts the people to remember, when times are good, that God is the one who brought these blessings.

The LORD your God (verse 14) is described more fully in the following verses (through verse 16).

The wilderness is described as *great and terrible* (NRSV) or *vast and dreadful* (NIV). The generation to whom Moses is speaking knows this wilderness experience only by reputation, not firsthand. The poisonous snakes are those that bit the people in the wilderness on account of their lack of faith. (See Numbers 21:6-9.) The water from the rock episode is described in Numbers 20. In the original narrative, Moses brought forth water from a rock after the people complained about being thirsty.

The positive and negative sides of future life in Canaan are both discussed in this passage. If the people remember God and obey the commandments, life will be good. If, however, they are not obedient, the result is clear. They will perish (verses 19-20).

God's Presence with Israel (9:1-5)

The introductory words *Hear, O Israel* identify this as a new section. The Israelites will soon cross over the Jordan.

Moses makes the point that the cities and the peoples

they will encounter will be mighty indeed. And they will conquer these people. But they must constantly remember that it is not their strength that will bring these victories about, but rather the hand of God. God will bring about victory on their behalf not because the Israelites have been a faithful people. Rather, God's motivation is the wickedness of the people who are already inhabiting the land.

God's Presence in History (9:6–10:11)

This section is a first-person narrative by Moses of the incident of the golden calf (narrated earlier in Exodus 32). However, the present account adds an element of judgment, that can be seen throughout the narrative.

According to verse 7, the Israelites have been stubborn and rebellious since they left Egypt many years earlier. Verse 8 mentions an incident at Horeb where the people *aroused* (NIV) or *provoked* (NRSV) *the LORD to wrath.*

In verses 9-11 Moses momentarily stops chastising the people to recite a short history, involving mainly the events at Mount Sinai.

In verses 12-21, Moses moves to a retelling of the episode of the golden calf. In this account, God is the one who discovers the sin and informs Moses of what the people have done. Verse 17 gives Moses' reaction when he sees the people's sin. He breaks the *two tablets* (on which the Ten Commandments were written). For forty days he neither eats nor drinks, presumably to atone for what the people have done. The tablets are useless now, since they represent the covenant, which has just been made and is now broken. Then Moses crushes the molten calf and throws the dust into the water.

Verses 22-24 list other similar acts of disobedience on the part of the people. The incident at Taberah is narrated in Numbers 11:1-3; the incident at Massah is found also in Exodus 17:1-7; the events at Kibroth-hattaavah are also narrated in Numbers 11:31-34.

Verse 23 speaks of the sending of the spies into Canaan, which was narrated earlier in Numbers 13–14.

In verses 25-29, Moses intercedes on behalf of the people. Moses reminds God of the deliverance from Egypt and the promises made to the patriarchs, and encourages God to have the same benevolent attitude now.

Chapter 10 begins with a retelling by Moses of his second ascent onto the sacred mountain. God wants Moses to make a second set of tablets like the one Moses broke in anger, as well as an ark that will be used to hold the tablets. Moses does as God asks. (See 1 Kings 8:9, where the ark containing the tablets is mentioned.)

Verses 6-9 are an editorial addition, indicated by the fact that they appear in parentheses in the Revised Standard Version. These verses mention part of the itinerary when Israel was wandering in the wilderness. The places mentioned, as well as their order, are different from the account given in Numbers 33. This list of places in which the Israelites stopped is probably occasioned by the mention of the ark in verse 2. This short passage explains how the ark was transported during the wandering of the Israelites in the wilderness.

In verses 10-11, God gives marching orders to Moses and the Israelites.

God Wants Faithfulness and Obedience (10:12-22)

Verses 12-13 repeat a famous exhortation to the people of Israel about what God requires of them. Comparable advice is given by the prophet Micah to his audience (see Micah 6:6-8). Moses makes the point that God could have chosen anyone in heaven or on earth, but God has chosen the Israelites.

Circumcise the foreskin of your heart (verse 16) means to dedicate one's heart to God. This image is reminiscent of Jeremiah's new covenant that will be written on the hearts of faithful Israelites (see Jeremiah 31:31-34).

In verses 18-19, Moses reminds the people of their special responsibilities toward certain members of society. Specifically, they are to treat the sojourner among them with special care because they were once sojourners themselves, in Egypt.

Seventy persons (verse 22): See Exodus 1:5.

God Demands Loyalty to the Covenant (11:1-25)

In this section, Moses continues to exhort the people to obedience, based on the evidence of what God has done for them in the past. The deliverance from Egypt described in verses 2-4 is narrated in Exodus 13–14. The story of Dathan and Abiram (verse 6) is told also in Numbers 16.

In verses 10-12, Moses makes a distinction between Egypt and Canaan, the Promised Land. The main difference is that Canaan is not irrigated as Egypt is, by the Nile River. But God will water the new land, nevertheless.

According to verse 14, God will provide early rain (in October, since the new year began in September), and later rain (in April).

Because life will be so good in the Promised Land (verse 16), the people will be tempted to worship other gods out of complacence. If that happens, Moses warns that there will be no water at all.

Verses 18-25 summarize this entire section. The people are to pass on these words from generation to generation. Verse 24 gives the boundaries of the Promised Land (the *western sea* refers to the Mediterranean Sea, to the west of Canaan).

A Blessing and a Curse (11:26-32)

In this section, two possibilities are offered to the Israelites. The decision rests on obedience to the covenant. Two mountains are mentioned, one for the blessing and one for the curse. Both mountains are located near Shechem in the central hill country, on the west side of the Jordan River.

An accompanying ceremony is implied but not mentioned directly. Deuteronomy 27 mentions a ceremony that takes place at Shechem involving the same two mountains.

§ § § § § § §

The Message of Deuteronomy 8–11

§ A successful life in the land of Canaan depends on the people's obedience to the commandments, and on their refraining from being corrupted by the influences of Canaanite religious practices.

§ God will continue to act on Israel's behalf; the proof is in what God has accomplished in the past.

§ At times God tests the quality of Israel's faith by causing the chosen people to endure suffering.

§ The Israelites must never think that victory over an enemy is their own doing. They must always realize that God's hand is at work on their behalf.

§ God will never forsake the covenant made with the patriarchs.

§ The people of Israel constantly have a choice before them. They can choose either blessing or curse.

§ § § § § § §

Deuteronomy 12–15

Introduction to These Chapters

These chapters are central to the message of the book
of Deuteronomy. Chapter 12 focuses on the centralization
of worship in the sanctuary. This section also includes
more exhortation concerning the worship of other gods,
and advice on how to live once the people become settled
in their new land.

Deuteronomy 12–15 may be outlined as follows.
  I. Worship Regulations (12:1-32)
     A. Where to bring burnt offerings (12:1-14)
     B. Appropriate animal sacrifices (12:15-28)
     C. Conclusion (12:29-32)
 II. Serving Other Gods (13:1-18)
     A. Dealing with false prophets (13:1-5)
     B. Dealing with others (13:6-18)
III. Clean and Unclean Foods (14:1-29)
     A. What the people may eat (14:1-20)
     B. Annual offerings to God (14:21-29)
 IV. Living in Community (15:1-23)
     A. The year of jubilee (15:1-11)
     B. Regulations about slaves (15:12-23)

Where to Bring Burnt Offerings (12:1-14)

Chapter 12 begins a lengthy section of the book in
which Moses speaks to the people concerning legal
matters (through chapter 26). This longer section is

appropriately introduced by the words in verse 1: *These are the statutes and ordinances* (NRSV) . . . . or *decrees and laws* (NIV).

The central idea of this chapter, the centralization of worship in a single location, is repeated three times in different ways. Each time the statement is made it is followed by discussion: verse 2 (discussion in verses 3-7), verse 8 (discussion in verses 9-12), and verse 13 (discussion in verse 14).

In verses 2-7, the point is made that not only must the Israelites not worship at the cultic shrines built by the Canaanites. They must also destroy all these shrines, along with their altars, pillars, and *Asherah* (NIV) or *sacred poles* (NRSV).

The place which the LORD *your God* will choose (verse 5) will eventually become the city of Jerusalem under the leadership of King David, two or three hundred years hence.

Verse 6 mentions various types of offerings that are to be brought to the central place once it is established. See also Numbers 28–29 and Leviticus 27.

Verses 8-12 form the second admonition and discussion. Verse 8 repeats verse 2, warning against worship in local Canaanite shrines. In those places, everyone does as he or she desires. The specific instructions in verse 11 repeat those in verse 6.

Verses 13-14 repeat the admonition a third time.

Appropriate Animal Sacrifices (12:15-28)

This section contains rules about which animals are to be eaten and which ones are to be sacrificed. Similar regulations were also given earlier in Leviticus 17, but these earlier laws are now adjusted in light of the fact that there will be only one place for these sacrifices to be made.

According to verse 15, although sacrifices are to be made at only one place, the slaughter of animals for purposes of food can take place anywhere. (The *gazelle* and the *deer* are game animals). Only the blood of these animals cannot be eaten. (Leviticus 17:10-14 explains that blood contains life and therefore is never to be eaten.)

Verse 17 states that the Israelites cannot eat things that are holy within their own towns, meaning things that are dedicated to God. These things must be brought to the central sanctuary and eaten there.

Verses 20-27 repeat earlier admonitions to the effect that (1) the people may eat appropriate meat in their own towns, but (2) they must not eat the blood of these animals, and (3) they must bring what has been dedicated to God to the central sanctuary.

Conclusion (12:29-32)

In these verses, chapter 12 concludes with a general warning against worshiping other gods once the people become settled in Canaan. *Detestable* (NIV) or *abhorent* (NRSV) *things* are specifically mentioned that take place in Canaanite cultic ritual, such as human sacrifice.

Verse 32 could be either a concluding statement to the section that has preceded or an introduction to what follows. In some versions, this verse is the first verse in chapter 13.

Dealing with False Prophets (13:1-5)

In chapter 13, the writer is concerned with the hypothetical situation in which the statement might be made to the chosen people: *Let us follow other gods* (verses 2, 6, and 13). Three scenarios are portrayed in which this statement might be made. Each time the enticement is offered by a different person or group of persons.

First, the statement is made by a false prophet. Often the test of a prophet in Israel was whether he could provide a sign of his authority. According to verse 3, if such a sign is offered, along with the invitation to *follow other gods*, the people are to recognize that God is testing them. The punishment for such a prophet is death.

Dealing with Others (13:6-18)

In this section two other scenarios are mentioned. First, a close friend or relative encourages someone to *follow other gods*. Again the appropriate answer is clearly No, and the punishment is severe: death by stoning.

The second scenario in this section involves a hypothetical situation in which a whole city has decided to turn to idol worship (verses 12-18). In this case, no direct invitation needs to be made to an individual. Whoever even hears of such a town is to destroy it and put its spoil under the ban (that is, dedicate the captured goods to God).

What the People May Eat (14:1-20)

Verses 1-2 are a separate section in which a certain Canaanite custom related to mourning the dead is prohibited (verse 1) and the reason given (verse 2).

Verses 3-20 contain a list of all kinds of animals that are considered to be clean and therefore appropriate for eating. Also, those animals considered to be unclean are listed. The list falls into three parts: mammals (verses 1-8), fish (verses 9-10), and birds (verses 11-20).

These lists probably existed previously and were used by the priests, who were responsible for such matters. A similar list is found in Leviticus 11.

Sometimes the English translations of Hebrew words for the various animals are difficult, especially when the Hebrew word is used only a few times in the Old Testament. Also, the reasons given for uncleanness among these animals may seem rather arbitrary, but unfortunately, no explanations are provided.

Annual Offerings to God (14:21-29)

Verse 21 is independent of what precedes and follows it; it could have been part of the previous section. This regulation concerning not eating anything that *dies of itself* (NRSV) or *is already dead* (NIV) is probably related to the fact that if an animal dies of itself, its blood is not poured out on the ground, but is allowed to drain onto the ground. Boiling a kid in its mother's milk is prohibited elsewhere (see Exodus 23:19, for example). Evidently cooking meat in this way was part of Canaanite cultic ritual.

Verses 22-29 contain regulations concerning the annual payment of tithes at the central sanctuary. Such tithing was relatively easy for those persons who lived near the sanctuary. But for persons living in the outlying areas, additional rules were needed. In those cases, the tithes were to be turned in for money, which was then brought to the sanctuary at a later time and spent appropriately.

Verses 27-29 are a reminder of the responsibility of caring for the Levites and other members of society who have no land of their own. Every three years, the tithe goes to these persons who are living in the various towns (rather than going to the central sanctuary).

The Year of Jubilee (15:1-11)

This year of jubilee, or year of release, is discussed at several points within the Old Testament legal material. In Exodus 23:10-11 it concerns agriculture: There will be six years of working the fields, and on the seventh year they will lie fallow. The poor among the people will be allowed to eat from what the fields produce during that year.

In Leviticus 25:1-7, the context for this subject is also agricultural. But there the purpose of the seventh year is not to provide food for the poor, but to allow the land to rejuvenate itself.

In the present passage in Deuteronomy, the context is not agricultural, but economic and social. In the seventh year, all creditors will release the debts owed to them.

The one exception involves foreigners—persons may still exact debts from them.

The ultimate goal of the jubilee year is that there will be no poor people living in the covenant community. Verse 11, however, adds a note of realism. The poor will remain among the people, but the ultimate goal is that everyone in the community is taken care of.

Regulations About Slaves (15:12-23)

Verses 12-18 relate to Exodus 21:2-11, which also states rules concerning slavery. The laws Israel enforced concerning slavery were governed by the fact that the Israelites were once slaves in Egypt, and that experience should carry over to their treatment of their own slaves.

Verses 19-23 are based on an older law requiring the sacrifice of all first-born to God (see Exodus 13:2). This older law is here adapted for use when there is a central sanctuary. First-born animals are to be taken annually to the sanctuary and eaten there. Also, no blemished animals are to be sacrificed (verse 21). Blemished animals may be eaten at home, however, as long as the blood is poured out on the ground.

§ § § § § § §

The Message of Deuteronomy 12–15

§ There is only one sanctuary in which it is appropriate for Israelites to worship God. This phenomenon of centralized worship was the most effective way to guard against the pagan influences the people would inevitably encounter as they settled in the land of Canaan.

§ No enticement from any person or group of persons should influence an Israelite to worship any other god besides Yahweh, Israel's God.

§ Those who encourage others to forsake God and follow other gods are to be cut off from the community (killed).

§ Special provisions are made for certain members of Israelite society, so their needs are cared for. The Israelites who have land and can produce food must share their goods with those who are less fortunate then they.

§ § § § § § §

PART FIFTEEN Deuteronomy 16–19

Introduction to These Chapters

These four chapters continue the long sermonic section related to laws and regulations that will govern the people as they settle in the land of Canaan. The present section includes regulations concerning the observance of feasts and festivals, the administration of justice, the rights of the Levites, the proper worship of God, and the cities of refuge.

Here is an outline of these chapters.
I. Festival Celebrations (16:1-22)
   A. The feast of the Passover (16:1-8)
   B. The feast of Weeks (16:9-12)
   C. The feast of Booths (16:13-15)
   D. Summary statements (16:16-22)
II. Laws Concerning Justice (17:1-20)
   A. Concerning idolatry (17:1-7)
   B. Concerning difficult cases (17:8-13)
   C. Concerning the king (17:14-20)
III. Treatment of the Priests (18:1-22)
IV. Cities of Refuge (19:1-21)
   A. The cities are established (19:1-14)
   B. The testimony of witnesses (19:15-21)

The Feast of the Passover (16:1-8)

The calendar of feasts, which is the subject of chapter 16, is given also in Numbers 28–29, Leviticus 23, and portions of the book of Exodus. Verses 1-8 contain regulations concerning the feast of the Passover and Unleavened Bread. According to an earlier law (see Numbers 28:16-25), sacrifices could be made locally to celebrate this festival. Here, however, they must be offered at the central sanctuary (*the place which the LORD will choose*, verse 2).

The observation of this festival will take place in the month of *Abib*, which is the month in which the original Exodus from Egypt took place (the event which this festival commemorates).

The festival is to last seven days, during which the people are to eat unleavened bread. The unleavened bread symbolizes the haste in which the people left Egypt, since they did not have time to let their bread rise. Verse 5 makes the adjustment clear—offerings may be made only at the central sanctuary, not in individual towns.

Verse 8 states that the total number of days in the festival was seven, with the final day being a day of solemn assembly.

The Feast of Weeks (16:9-12)

The feast of Weeks celebrates the spring corn harvest, and is held in June (seven weeks after the harvest begins, according to verse 9). The feast is also mentioned in Exodus 23:16 (where it is called the feast of harvest), Exodus 34:22, Leviticus 23:15-16, and Numbers 28:26.

The Feast of Booths (16:13-15)

This feast is also called the feast of the ingathering, and the feast of tabernacles (in the King James Version). It is celebrated in the fall as a thanksgiving for the fall harvest. It, too, is a seven-day festival.

This feast is also discussed in Leviticus 23:33-43, where the original meaning is given. The booths symbolize the transitory nature of Israelite existence while the people were wandering in the wilderness.

Summary Statements (16:16-22)

In summary, the Israelites were to observe three festivals at three times during each year, one week at a time. Males only were to appear at the central sanctuary during these times, bearing the appropriate sacrifices. A similar summary statement is found in Exodus 23:17.

According to verses 18-20, an established community has need of judges and officers to keep the peace among its members. Remember that this material from the mouth of Moses has been placed in the context of last-minute instructions before the people cross the Jordan to take over the land of Canaan. Actually, most of this material (in Deuteronomy) is written in such a way that it assumes an already-established community. It is probably the product of a long tradition that found its final form during the sixth century B.C.

Verses 21-22 prohibit the construction of Canaanite altars.

Concerning Idolatry (17:1-7)

Actually these verses are a continuation of the thought begun in 16:21, God's objection to idol worship. According to verse 1, no blemished animal can be sacrificed to God. (See 15:21-23 for an indication of how these animals are to be dealt with.)

Verses 2-7 make the point that the punishment for idol worship is death. But there must be more than one witness to the idol worship in order for the person to be found guilty. If the witnesses are actually the ones to begin the stoning, then the evil brought about by the sin will be erased.

Concerning Difficult Cases (17:8-13)

Cases requiring difficult decisions or involving serious crimes will be judged by a special group of people in the location of the central sanctuary. This group of people will consist of the priests and the judge officiating at the time. Their decision is final and must be adhered to.

Again, this regulation assumes the presence of an office of judge, which did not exist in Israel until the community had settled in the area (about 1100 B.C.).

Concerning the King (17:14-20)

At the time Moses was speaking to the people as they were encamped on the east side of the Jordan, there were no kings yet in Israel. But Moses is speaking as though he is looking to the future (see verse 14). (See the comments on 16:16-22.)

The event described in verses 14-15 (Israel's request for a king) did happen during the time of Samuel (see 1 Samuel 8:4-22). According to verse 15, the king must be a native Israelite. The prohibition against horse trading (verse 16) assumes a knowledge of King Solomon's actions in this area (see 1 Kings 10:26-29).

This law (verse 18) refers to the laws in the book of Deuteronomy.

According to verse 20, the king is not above the law; he must observe legal and cultic regulations just like any other Israelite.

Treatment of the Priests (18:1-22)

Verses 1-8 discuss the rights of the Levites within the Israelite community. The Levites are identified in verse 1 as *the whole tribe of Levi*. They have no inheritance of their own (see Numbers 18, and the commentary on that chapter). Some of these Levites were located at the central sanctuary, and some were living within individual towns. According to verses 6-8, any Levite living in one of the towns may come to the central sanctuary at any time and operate as a full-fledged priest while he is there.

The meaning of *sale of family possessions* (verse 8) is unclear.

Verses 9-22 discuss laws regarding prophecy and prophetic speech. Verse 9 lists Canaanite practices that are abominations to God, including child sacrifice as well as various forms of divination. Verse 15 promises an Israelite counterpart to these Canaanite soothsayers, a prophet who is *like me*, that is, like Moses. (Moses was the first prophet and served as a model for all future prophets.)

Verse 16 defines the role of the prophet as mediator between the people and God.

Verse 20 warns against false prophets. The test of a true prophet is future-oriented. If his words prove true at a later date, then the prophet is considered to be a true prophet of God.

The Cities Are Established (19:1-14)

The cities of refuge are first mentioned in Numbers 35, where their reason for existence is given. If a person has killed unintentionally, he needs a place of protection from his avenger (see the commentary on Numbers 35). Later, in Deuteronomy 4:41-43, three of these cities (those on the east side of the Jordan) are identified. According to verse 9, the rest of the six cities will be identified at a later date.

Verses 4-6 elaborate on the purpose of the cities of refuge, adding a specific example of unintentional killing.

Verses 11-13 make clear that a man who is guilty of intentional murder may be pursued inside a city of refuge, to guard against possible abuse of this form of protection.

A *boundary marker* (NRSV) or *stone* (NIV) (verse 14) refers to a property marker, which could not be removed from a person's property by anyone else.

The Testimony of Witnesses (19:15-21)

These verses repeat an earlier ruling that more than one witness was necessary to convict someone of a serious crime (see Deuteronomy 17:6; Numbers 35:30). False witness will be adjudicated between the accuser and the accused by a group of judges and priests. False witness, or false accusation, brings the same punishment that would have been given to the accused if he had been found guilty by the tribunal.

An eye for an eye (verse 21) is called the *lex talionis* (law of retaliation). It is discussed also in Leviticus 24:20 and Exodus 21:22-25. Although this law may sound harsh to our ears, it was originally intended to maintain a proper balance in the society as a whole.

§ § § § § § §

The Message of Deuteronomy 16–19

§ Certain festivals were designated for the Israelites to observe, in commemoration of their history and of God's involvement in it on their behalf.

§ A central sanctuary was set aside for the purpose of guarding against the possibility of pagan influences from the surrounding Canaanite culture once the Israelites were settled in the land of Canaan.

§ Certain Canaanite practices were specifically prohibited, such as child sacrifice, boiling a kid in its mother's milk, and various forms of divination.

§ The law of retaliation was set up to preserve a proper balance in society, not to promote harsh judgment and punishment among its members.

§ § § § § § §

Deuteronomy 20–23

Introduction to These Chapters

These chapters continue Moses' exhortation concerning regulations of the settled life in Canaan. This section contains regulations regarding holy war, laws concerning murder, concerning treatment of the Levites, and many other miscellaneous rules and regulations.

Deuteronomy 20–23 may be outlined as follows.
I. Regulations Concerning Holy War (20:1-20)
II. Other Laws and Regulations (21:1–23:25)
  A. Concerning murder (21:1-9)
  B. Concerning holy war (21:10-14)
  C. Concerning family matters (21:15-23)
  D. Concerning fellow Israelites (22:1-4)
  E. Miscellaneous laws (22:5-12)
  F. Concerning sexual relations (22:13-30)
  G. Concerning exclusions from the assembly (23:1-8)
  H. Miscellaneous laws (23:9-25)

Regulations Concerning Holy War (20:1-20)

Verses 1-20 look to the conquest of Canaan. These verses provide rules for the people to follow while engaging in these battles. First, and most important, the people are never to forget who is guiding them in battle. With the knowledge that God's hand is guiding the events, the people do not need to fear the strength of their enemies.

Verse 3 states that the priest is to address the soldiers right before the battle begins, reminding them that God is behind them, supporting them.

Verses 4-9 repeat a speech that is to be made by the officers, during the time of final preparations for battle. The officers are to remind the soldiers that certain circumstances release them from military service, even at this late stage. Why do such (seemingly unimportant) reasons exempt a person from service? Because the battle will be won not with numbers, but with the presence of God.

Verses 10-18 tell what to do with the goods and inhabitants of a captured city. If the city is not inhabited by Hittites, Amorites, Canaanites, Perizzites, Hivites, or Jebusites, then the Israelites may take the booty for themselves. If this city is inhabited by one of these peoples, the booty must be dedicated to God.

Verses 19-20 protect trees from indiscriminate destruction, since they are precious natural resources and can be used for food and weapons.

Concerning Murder (21:1-9)

This section details what happens when a murder takes place and the murderer is unidentified. According to Israelite law, all murder must be avenged. If the murderer is not known, steps are taken to identify the closest city. The elders of that city are then gathered to sacrifice a heifer. They literally "wash their hands of the matter" over the body of the slain animal.

Concerning Holy War (21:10-14)

These verses are an addendum to chapter 20. They contain more regulations that deal with holy war—these are concerned with women who are taken captive by Israelite soldiers. A woman who is captured is taken to the home of the Israelite man who wants her, and made to shave her head and cut her nails. The man is not allowed to have sexual relations with her for at least one month. After that time she may be sent away at any time, but she may not be sold by the man who took her captive.

Concerning Family Matters (21:15-23)

Verses 15-17 concern the inheritance rights of children. Since Israelite men could have more than one wife, rules were needed to govern the inheritance of his children by his various wives. Birth order is the absolute determinant. A man cannot favor one child over another, even if he favors that child's mother over his other wives. The rights of the first-born are the basis for the Jacob-Esau story (see Genesis 25:29-34).

Verses 18-21 discuss the relationship between parents and a rebellious son. The law here seems very harsh, but it reflects the commandment to honor one's parents. For sons that are uncontrollable, the parents have the recourse of appealing to the city elders for help. The elders can stone the boy to death for his rebellious behavior.

Verses 22-23 allow for hanging a criminal from a tree the first day after he is put to death. This was the ultimate humiliation, since in Israel proper burial is very important.

Concerning Fellow Israelites (22:1-4)

This law concerns looking out for the possessions of one's fellow Israelites. *Brother* (NIV) (verse 1) means close friend, *neighbor* (NRSV) as well as relative. See also Exodus 23:4-5.

Miscellaneous Laws (22:5-12)

This section contains laws which are basically unrelated to one another. First, men and women are to maintain the basic distinctions between their genders (verse 5). Second, the Israelites are to be kind to animals, especially mothers with their young (verses 6-7). Third, they are to place parapets on the roofs of their houses to guard against someone falling off. Fourth, the mixing of two or more things is prohibited. Three examples are given. *Be forfeited* (NRSV) can also be translated *become holy*. Fifth, the Israelites are to make tassels and put them on the four corners of a piece of cloth out of which a cloak is made (see Numbers 15:37-41).

Concerning Sexual Relations (22:13-30)

Verses 13-21 describe how to prove a young woman's virginity. This would need to be done in the case of a husband suspecting that his bride is not a virgin. If he suspects that she is not, he may demand a hearing in the presence of the elders of the city. The young woman's parents bring her, along with the bed coverings (*proof* (NIV) or *evidence* (NRSV) of her virginity, since if she is a virgin they will be covered with bloodstains). If the parents can produce tokens of her virginity, then the man is punished both physically and financially. He is also forced to keep the young woman as his wife.

If her parents cannot produce proof of her virginity, she is stoned to death.

Verses 22-30 contain five separate laws related to adultery. First, if a man (married or unmarried) has sexual relations with a married woman, they are both killed (verse 22). Second, if a woman is not yet married but she is engaged to be married, she is considered to be married so the penalty is the same as if she were (verses 23-24).

Third, if a man rapes a betrothed woman, only he is punished. However, the crime must take place in the open country, where her cries for help could not be heard (verses 25-27). Fourth, if a young woman who is not engaged is raped, the man must pay her father fifty shekels. This amount is equivalent to the bride's price that would have been paid for her if she had been a virgin. Now she cannot exact that price when betrothed, since she is defiled (verses 28-29). Fifth, sexual relations between a man and his stepmother are prohibited (verse 30).

Concerning Exclusions from the Assembly (23:1-8)

These verses contain a list of those excluded from the *assembly of the* LORD (whenever the congregation gathers for any cultic ritual). Three kinds of people are excluded, according to these verses: eunuchs (verse 1; see Leviticus 21:17-23), bastards (verse 2; see Leviticus 18:6-18), and Ammonites and Moabites. Edomites are allowed to enter the assembly, however, as well as Egyptians.

Miscellaneous Laws (23:9-25)

Verses 9-14 relate to conduct during holy war. Soldiers are to keep themselves clean at all times. If they become unclean for any reason, they are to remove themselves from the camp for a day. They are also to observe basic rules of personal hygiene in order to keep their camp clean, both ritually and physically.

Verses 15-16 concern a runaway slave. Such a person is not to be turned over to his master, but is to be protected wherever he goes.

According to verses 17-18, cult prostitutes are prohibited among the people of Israel. A *dog* (verse 18) is another name for a male prostitute.

Verses 19-20 repeat the regulation found in Exodus 22:25. No one is to lend money for the purpose of exacting interest. Foreigners, however, must pay interest to Israelites if it is requested.

Verses 21-23 discuss the making of vows (see Leviticus 27). At all costs, vows must be upheld. Verses 24-25 provide for goodwill among neighbors. When Israelites go into the gardens of their neighbors, they should expect to eat their fill of grapes. However, they may not take advantage of this opportunity by filling up containers with fruit. The same guideline holds true for grain.

§ § § § § § §

The Message of Deuteronomy 20–23

§ Israel's God, who accompanied the people when they left Egypt, will accompany them during the conquest of the Promised Land as well.

§ The numbers of soldiers that participate in the various battles that make up the conquest of the Promised Land are not important. What is important is the presence of God with the people as they go to war.

§ Many rules and regulations were necessary to enable a successful settled life in the land of Canaan.

§ Some of Israel's laws were strictly religious; others were humanitarian and helped the Israelites live harmoniously with one another.

§ Participation in the congregational worship of God was a privilege that was not granted to everyone.

§ § § § § § §

Deuteronomy 24–27

Introduction to These Chapters

These chapters deal with laws related to humanitarian matters. These laws cover such matters as divorce; making loans; treatment of slaves, widows, and sojourners; and personal disagreements. A major portion of Moses' second sermon (which began at chapter 5), is concluded in chapter 26. Chapter 27 describes a ceremony at which the covenant between God and Israel is renewed.

Here is an outline of Deuteronomy 24–27.
  I. Miscellaneous Laws (24:1–25:19)
 II. Concluding Statements (26:1-19)
III. A Covenant Ceremony (27:1-26)
      A. Introduction (27:1-14)
      B. Ritual of the curse (27:15-26)

Miscellaneous Laws (24:1–25:19)

This part of the book of Deuteronomy contains fifteen laws of various lengths and varying amounts of detail. In verses 1-4, a woman twice married and divorced cannot remarry her first husband because she is defiled. A *certificate of divorce* (verse 1) is a legal document containing the grounds for divorce (identifying the *indecency*).

According to verse 5, newly married men are exempt from military service for one year. Verse 6 states that no creditor can take a mill for a debt, since a mill is used to grind grain and grain is necessary to survive. The law in verse 7 states that no one can steal another human being and sell him (or her, presumably) into slavery.

Verses 8-9 concern leprosy, and legislate that this disease requires the observance of strict regulations (see Leviticus 13–14). Verses 10-13 state that it is unlawful to go inside a person's house to exact a loan payment. *Sleep with his pledge* (NIV) means to take his *garment* (NRSV) in payment for a loan.

According to verses 14-15, treatment of hired servants must be reasonable. Since they depend on the money they make for their livelihood, they must be paid each day before the sun goes down. Verse 16 states that no one can be killed for the sin of his parents or his children. Individuals are responsible for their own sins (unlike Numbers 16, where the whole households of Dathan and Abiram are punished for the sins of these two men).

Verses 17-18 concern the treatment of slaves, in accordance with the fact that the Israelites were once slaves themselves. According to verses 19-22, the excess harvest in the fields will go to the less fortunate members of society. Verses 1-3 of chapter 25 concern restrictions on physical punishment if one is determined to be guilty of a minor crime.

Verse 4 legislates humane treatment while using an ox for plowing one's fields.

Verses 5-10 concern the law of levirate marriage. According to this law, a dead man's brother is required to marry his brother's widow (his sister-in-law) in order to protect her.

Verses 11-12 are a rather harsh law that protects the genital organs of a man involved in a fight. Verses 13-16 are a prohibition against cheating in determining weights.

Verses 17-19 conclude this section with a reminder of the battle against the Amalekites (see Exodus 17:8-15).

Concluding Statements (26:1-19)

This chapter concludes a major portion of Moses' second of three sermons, which began in chapter 5.

According to verses 1-11, the first fruits must be offered at the central sanctuary when the people have settled in the land of Canaan. This offering will take place during the feast of Weeks, which celebrates the fall harvest. (See Deuteronomy 16:9-12.)

Evidently part of the ritual that accompanies this offering is the recitation of a historical creed (verses 5-9) that begins with the patriarchs and ends with the conquest of Canaan.

A wandering Aramean (verse 5) refers to Jacob, the father of the twelve tribes of Israel.

After the creed is recited, the offering is presented.

According to verses 12-15, the ritual of tithing is to take place every third year. This passage gives the words the tithers are to say (verses 13-15). These are words of assurance that the commandments have been obeyed and a request for a blessing.

Verses 16-19 conclude the larger section of statutes and ordinances that began in chapter 12. According to Moses, God has done three things: (1) commanded the people to obey the statutes and ordinances, (2) declared that the chosen people are God's possession, and (3) promised that the people will be holy to God. The people respond by declaring that they do indeed belong to God.

Introduction (27:1-14)

We know this is a new section in the narrative, because Moses is no longer speaking in the first person. This is a narrative about Moses, who commands the people (verse 2) to set up stones and write the law on them. They are to set up these stones on Mount Ebal, which is near the city of Shechem. These stones are to be set up alongside an altar, which is to be built of stones that are uncut.

After making these preparations, the people are to

offer appropriate sacrifices upon the altar, and write the law upon the stones (as commanded previously).

Verses 9-10 summarize the command to *hear* (NRSV) or *listen* (NIV) and *obey* the commandments, statutes, and ordinances.

According to verses 11-14, after the people cross the Jordan, half the tribes are to ascend Mount Ebal (the mountain of cursing) and half the tribes are to ascend Mount Gerizim (the mountain of blessing). The twelve tribes are listed, according to which mountain they are to ascend. Note that the tribe of Levi is listed, instead of the two tribes of Ephraim and Manasseh (they are replaced by their father, Joseph). The listing of Levi as a tribe signifies a very ancient list that was inserted by the writer at this point in the narrative. After Israel's earliest history, Levi was no longer listed as one of the tribes.

The division of the tribes into tribes for blessing and tribes for cursing seems to be arbitrary.

Ritual of the Curse (27:15-26)

Twelve different kinds of people are cursed in this section. One curse is given for each tribe. The Levites read the curse and all the people respond by saying *Amen*. Almost all these curses are found elsewhere in the Old Testament legal material. Again, we have a very ancient curse list that has been incorporated into this narrative.

The blessings that originally formed the counterpart to this curse list have evidently been lost in the process of transmission of the text. Some blessings do, however, appear in the next chapter.

§ § § § § § §

The Message of Deuteronomy 24–27

§ God intends to take care of the unfortunate members of Israelite society, so laws are provided that protect their welfare.

§ Individuals within the community are responsible for their own sins.

§ Sometimes Israelite law, which was set up to maintain balance and harmonious living conditions in the community, sounds harsh to our modern ears.

§ Israel's history is a part of what the people have become.

§ The Israelites by this time have come to believe that God is the only God, who designated them as the chosen people.

§ § § § § § §

Deuteronomy 28–30

Introduction to These Chapters

Deuteronomy 28–30 contain the third and final sermon of Moses to the people before they cross the Jordan into the Promised Land. First, however, Moses concludes his earlier sermon, begun in chapter 5. Then he proceeds to exhort the people to obey the covenant made with God, and warns them of the punishment that they will incur if they do not obey.

Deuteronomy 28–30 may be outlined as follows.
I. Conclusion (to Moses' second sermon) (28:1-68)
  A. The blessings and their explanations (28:1-14)
  B. The curses and their explanations (28:15-46)
  C. God summons the enemy (28:47-68)
II. Moses' Third Address (29:1–30:20)
  A. A description of the covenant (29:1-29)
  B. Israel in exile (30:1-10)
  C. The people have a choice (30:11-20)

The Blessings and Their Explanations (28:1-14)

This is the last chapter of Moses' address to the people which began in chapter 5.

Verses 1-6 list six blessings that will accompany obedience to the commandments, statutes, and ordinances. Verse 1 is an introductory statement in which God promises to set Israel over all nations.

Verses 3-6 contain the actual blessings. They are short and to the point.

1. *Blessed shall you be in the city*
2. *Blessed shall you be in the field*
3. *Blessed shall be the fruit of your body*
4. *Blessed shall be your basket and your kneading-trough*
5. *Blessed shall you be when you come in*
6. *Blessed shall you be when you go out*

Verses 7-14 discuss the meaning of these blessings. Verse 7 refers to the general statement made in verse 1 concerning Israel's enemies. Verse 8 refers to the second blessing. Verses 9-10 refer to verse 1. Verse 11 refers to blessing three. Verse 12 refers to blessing number four. Verses 13-14 form a general conclusion.

The Curses and Their Explanations (28:15-46)

In addition to the twelve curses given in chapter 27, six more are given here to correspond to the six blessings in verses 3-6. Commentators have long noted that more attention is given to the curses and their explanations (verses 15-46) than to the blessings (verses 1-14).

Verse 15 introduces the corresponding curses, which are as follows.

1. *Cursed shall you be in the city*
2. *Cursed shall you be in the field*
3. *Cursed shall be your basket and your kneading-trough*
4. *Cursed shall be the fruit of your body*
5. *Cursed shall you be when you come in*
6. *Cursed shall you be when you go out*

Note that curses number 3 and 4 are reversed from the order of the blessings; otherwise the blessings and the curses are the same.

Verses 20-46 comment on the six curses. It is difficult to connect most of these comments with any particular curse, but the general impression is that all kinds of horrors await the people if they are disobedient. The people will be defeated by their enemies, they will endure plagues, droughts, personal humiliation, insanity, and blindness, among other things. They will be subdued by an unknown foreign nation (verses 36-37), probably a reference to the Babylonian defeat and captivity some 700 years later.

Some normal situations will be reversed—for example, the sojourner will rule over the native Israelite (verse 44).

God Summons the Enemy (28:47-68)

These verses are actually a continuation of the explanation of the curses that began in verse 20, but here the discussion is taken in a little different direction. This elaboration has to do with the circumstances surrounding the Babylonian exile, in 587 B.C. These verses were probably inserted when the book was put into its final form in the sixth century B.C. (right after the exile began, and when these circumstances were fresh on the mind of the writer or writers who compiled the final form of the book).

Verse 48 paints a poignant picture of the people being led into captivity in chains. Apparently, the situation will become desperate; some gruesome details are provided in verses 54-57.

Verses 58-68 restate the situation and summarize. Verse 68 brings the people full circle. If they do not obey the commandments, they will end up back in Egypt, wiping out all that they have accomplished since they left there over a generation earlier. If they return to Egypt, their circumstances will be even worse than they were before.

A Description of the Covenant (29:1-29)

This chapter begins Moses' third sermon (the three sermons are found in chapters 1–4, 5–28, and 29–30). Verse 1 serves as an introduction to the next two chapters. In the Hebrew text, this verse is the last verse in the previous chapter.

This introduction mentions a covenant made in Moab, in addition to the one made earlier at Horeb (Sinai).

Actually, the covenant mentioned here is a renewal of the earlier covenant. This covenant in Moab is not mentioned anywhere else in the Old Testament.

Verses 2-9 are a recital of God's accomplishments in history, beginning with the deliverance from oppression in Egypt, moving through the wilderness experience and the defeat of Sihon and Og, to the taking of their territory east of the Jordan River.

Verses 10-15 are an invitation to accept the covenant; these verses repeat the summons given in 26:16-19.

Verses 16-28 continue Moses' speech about what may happen if the people reject the covenant at some time in the future. First, if an individual turns away from God and toward the gods of other nations, God would *blot out* his or her name (verse 20), in addition to other calamities that would come upon the people as a whole. Then when later generations question the origin of these calamities, they will be told that they are the result of the Israelites' worshiping other gods.

The phrase *this book* occurs several times in this passage (verses 20, 21, 27, and 29). The phrase refers to the Book of Deuteronomy itself. The references indicate that these particular verses are a later addition to the book.

Israel in Exile (30:1-10)

Here Moses sets his exhortation in the context of the future, and the people are asked to assume that the (Babylonian) Exile has already taken place. How will they feel? What will they do?

The people are exiled into a foreign nation (verse 1). They respond to their punishment by repenting, and returning to God (verse 2). God will respond in compassion (verse 3), and will gather the scattered people into one place (verses 4-5).

God will circumcise the heart of the people—a concept mentioned earlier by Moses (see Deuteronomy 10:16).

The people will then respond in faithfulness and obedience.

The People Have a Choice (30:11-20)

Where is this covenant (*commandment*) located? According to Moses, it is written on the hearts of the Israelites. According to verses 15-20, Israel must make an important decision. Two ways are before the people: the way of *life and prosperity*, and the way of *death and destruction* (NIV) or *adversity* (NIV). Obedience to God will result in the way of life; turning away from God will result in the way of death (verse 18).

Of these two choices, Moses exhorts the people to choose the way of life.

§ § § § § § §

The Message of Deuteronomy 28–30

§ Blessings and curses are both options for the Israelites, depending on their response to the covenant.

§ Events in the future (such as the Babylonian exile) are seen as a direct result of the people's disregard for the covenant.

§ Disobedience of the commandments will have disastrous results; obedience will bring a life of peace and prosperity.

§ God's actions in the past on Israel's behalf are proof that God will continue to act on behalf of the chosen people in the future.

§ § § § § § §

Deuteronomy 31–34

Introduction to These Chapters

Moses has now concluded his third sermon. These last four chapters in the book of Deuteronomy narrate the events during the final days of Moses' life. As they have been all through the book of Deuteronomy, the Israelites are encamped just east of the Jordan River, waiting to cross over into the Promised Land. These chapters contain Moses' final exhortation to obedience, a psalm contrasting God's faithfulness with the people's disobedience, Moses' final blessing on the people, and the story of Moses' death on Mount Nebo.

Here is an outline of these chapters.
I. Moses' Final Words to the People (31:1-29)
  A. Moses encourages the people (31:1-13)
  B. Joshua is commissioned (31:14-29)
II. The Song of Moses (31:30–32:47)
III. Moses Ascends Mount Nebo (32:48-52)
IV. Moses Blesses the People (33:1-29)
V. The Death of Moses (34:1-12)

Moses Encourages the People (31:1-13)

This section falls into two main parts. In verses 1-8, Moses gives final instructions to the people concerning obedience to the covenant. In verses 9-13, he legislates a ceremony to renew the covenant every seven years.

Moses informs the people that he is 120 years old, near

the end of his lifetime. Before he dies he wants to make certain the people understand what they are to do. He reminds the people that God had decided earlier that he would not be able to cross the Jordan into the Promised Land. In one version of that story God's decision was based on the unbelief of Moses (see Numbers 27:12-14). In another account, God decided that Moses would not cross the Jordan because of the sin of the people (see Deuteronomy 1:37-38).

According to verses 3-6, the people need not fear the struggles they are destined to encounter as they enter the Promised Land. The people, led by Joshua and God, will be victorious over their enemies just as they were victorious over Sihon and Og.

In verses 7-8, Moses commissions Joshua as the new leader over the people. These same words are repeated in Joshua 1:1-9.

Verses 9-13 depict a covenant ceremony which is to be held every seven years when the people become settled in the Promised Land. The ceremony is to take place during the feast of Booths, which is held during the autumn as a thanksgiving ceremony for the fall harvest.

The seventh year is the *year of remission* (NRSV) or *the year for cancelling debts* (NIV) (verse 10); it is discussed more fully in Deuteronomy 15. In this year of release, the people are to be summoned together in one place (the central sanctuary) and the law is to be read in their hearing. By *law* is meant the book of Deuteronomy, which Moses is said to have written and given to the priests.

Joshua Is Commissioned (31:14-29)

Whereas Moses spoke to Joshua previously and informed him of his task (see verses 7-8), here God commissions him officially (see also Numbers 27:12-23). The word *commission* is actually used (verse 14). Moses and Joshua stand side by side in the tabernacle, and God appears in a pillar of cloud. The cloud is necessary because, according to tradition, no one was allowed to see the face of God and live (see Exodus 33:20).

In verses 16-22 God gives the final instruction to Moses, since Moses is now near death (*rest with your fathers*) (NIV) or *lie down with your ancestors* (NRSV). God predicts that after the death of Moses the people will fall back to worshiping other gods. God will become angry, and withdraw from them to punish them.

In verse 19, Moses is commanded to write a song that will remind the people of their disobedience. Since it will be taught to their descendants, the people of Israel will remember it forever.

Verse 22 reports that Moses does write the song that God commanded him to write. The song is found in Deuteronomy 32.

Verse 23 reports that God commissions Joshua, as was alluded to in verse 16.

Verses 24-27 restate God's desire concerning the preservation of the law for future generations (see verses 9-13).

Verse 30 introduces the song that follows in chapter 32.

The Song of Moses (31:30–32:47)

Listen, *O heavens* (verse 1) introduces this song of Moses. Verses 1-3 appeal to the listeners to accept the words of the song in the right spirit.

Verses 4-6 extol God as a rock which never changes. God's devotion to Israel is constant, in contrast to the chosen people, who are *a perverse* (NRSV) or *warped* (NIV) *and crooked* generation.

Verses 7-14 list God's past accomplishments on Israel's behalf. God originally divided all peoples into groups, and then chose the people of Israel to be God's special possession among all the other peoples (verse 7-9). Then God took the chosen people and cared for them as an eagle cares for its young (verses 10-14).

But what did Israel do? Israel rebelled against God

(verses 15-18). The people became complacent and went after other gods.

In verses 19-27, God responds in anger to the people's disobedience. God withdraws (*I will hide my face*). God is so angry that the divine wrath will cause the foundations of the earth to burn (verse 22). Verses 23-27 are a graphic description of what will happen to the people if they disobey.

According to verses 28-33, the nations are totally perverse, because they do not know God. Their help comes from gods who ultimately have no power. *Sodom and Gomorrah* are two cities known for the perversity of their inhabitants (see Genesis 19).

Verses 34-43 state that God will have vengeance against these other nations, and that day is coming soon. No matter how angry God becomes with Israel, God will ultimately come to the aid of the Israelites in their battles against these other nations.

The phrase *I am . . . he* in verse 39 is called a *divine self-predication formula,* in which God is revealed as unique from the gods of other nations. What follows this formula expresses the idea that everything that happens is under the ultimate control of Israel's God.

Verses 44-47 conclude the song. Joshua is called Hoshea (verse 44), as he is elsewhere in the Old Testament. Moses concludes this section with a reminder to the people to obey the commandments given to them.

Moses Ascends Mount Nebo (32:48-52)

God commands Moses to ascend Mount Nebo, which is in the mountain range called *Abarim* (on the east side of the Jordan River). God explains why Moses is to view the land but is not allowed to cross the river to tread on the ground. He was guilty of unbelief during the period of the wilderness wandering (see Numbers 20:10-15).

Moses Blesses the People (33:1-29)

In this chapter, Moses blesses the people of Israel before his death, just as Jacob did some years earlier (see Genesis 49). These blessings are cast in the form of predictions of the future, and may have actually been written at a later date and ascribed to Moses. Only eleven tribes are mentioned in this list; perhaps the tribe of Simeon had already died out by this time. (Remember that the numbers of this tribe decreased drastically in between the two censuses that were taken in the Book of Numbers, from 43,650 to 22,200.)

Verse 1 introduces the whole chapter, and verses 2-5 offer praise to God who came to Israel at Sinai and elsewhere.

Jeshurun (verse 5) is another name for Israel, whose meaning is uncertain.

Verse 6 is directed to *Reuben*. Moses requests that this tribe not be allowed to die out. Apparently the Reubenites had lost many members. Note that the tribe of Gad, which is also located in the territory east of the Jordan, is blessed in the same way (see verse 20).

In verse 7, Moses pleads for help from the other tribes on behalf of *Judah*, who is being threatened by an unnamed enemy. Verses 8-11 concern the tribe of Levi. That tribe is given the duties of the priesthood (see also Numbers 3). *Urim* and *Thummim* are sacred lots used to determine the will of God when a decision needs to be made.

Verse 12 is a blessing on the tribe of *Benjamin*, who apparently had a favored place among the tribes. Benjamin was the youngest son of Jacob and Rachel (see Genesis 35:16-18).

Verses 13-17 are Moses' blessing on the tribe of *Joseph*. Note that this tribe is not divided into the tribes of Ephraim and Manasseh (although they are mentioned in verse 17), since the Levites are listed as a tribe. (See the commentary on Numbers 1:47-54.) For Joseph, Moses wishes plentiful, good harvests and strong armies. Joseph is called a *prince among his brothers*, indicating his elevated status.

Him that dwelt in the burning bush (NIV) or *the one who dwells on Sinai* (NRSV) (verse 16) is probably a reference to God and the events in Exodus 3.

Verses 18-19 contain the blessing on *Zebulun* and *Issachar*. The Mediterranean Sea will provide their affluence for them, in the form of trade.

In verses 20-21 Moses blesses the tribe of *Gad*, who occupied the territory east of the Jordan but who nevertheless took part in the conquest of the land on the west side (see Numbers 32).

Verse 22 blesses *Dan*, who has located in the territory of Bashan in the northeast portion of the country.

In verse 23 Moses blesses the tribe of *Naphtali*. *Lake* refers to the Sea of Galilee.

The tribe of *Asher* (verses 24-25) is strong and prosperous, a favorite among his brothers.

Verses 26-29 offer praise to God, thus concluding the poem the same way it began in verses 2-6. This part of the poem is addressed to God in the second person.

The Death of Moses (34:1-12)

Here Moses ascends Mount Nebo, as he was told to do earlier (see Numbers 27:12; Deuteronomy 3:27). Mount Nebo is called *Pisgah* as well. From this point Moses can look out across the Promised Land. Verses 3-4 elaborate on all the territory Moses can see from there.

According to verse 6, God secretly buries Moses somewhere in the land of Moab.

In verse 9, Joshua is commissioned as Moses' successor (see also Numbers 27:18-23).

Verses 10-12 are a fitting conclusion to the book, since they extol Moses as the greatest prophet in the history of Israel.

§ § § § § § §

The Message of Deuteronomy 31–34

§ Receiving the land of promise is imminent for the Israelites. The taking of this land represents the fulfillment of God's promise of land made to the patriarchs.

§ The people are to enter into the conquest of Canaan, sure in the knowledge that their God is with them.

§ After the death of Moses, God will not leave the people without a leader. God will appoint another leader (Joshua) to take his place.

§ The God of Israel will not tolerate the worship of any other gods. This idol-worship will be a temptation for the people as they become settled and complacent in their new land.

§ God represents stability and dependability in the face of the faithlessness and disobedience of the chosen people.

§ § § § § § §

Glossary of Terms

Aaron: The brother of Moses, father of Nadab and Abihu.

Abihu: One of the sons of Aaron. He and his brother Nadab sinned by offering inappropriate sacrifices.

Abiram: Along with his brother Dathan, he led Korah's rebellion against Moses in the wilderness.

Admah: One of the cities of the valley, which was destroyed along with Sodom and Gomorrah.

Akrabbim: A mountainous region in southern Palestine.

Amalekites: Members of a nomadic tribe that was descended from Esau. The tribe waged war with the Israelites from time to time during their history.

Amaw: The territory where Balaam was located when he was summoned by Balak, king of Moab.

Ammonites: The people of Ammon, a territory east of the Jordan River.

Amorites: The people dwelling in the land of Amurru, which is of uncertain location but may have been the same as Syria.

Amram: A son of Kohath, father of Moses, Aaron, and Miriam.

Anakim: Descendants of Anak, who lived in Canaan prior to the Israelites arrival there. These people were known for their large size.

Ar: A Moabite city located in the northern part of Moab; perhaps it was the capital of this region.

Arabah: The region in Palestine that extends from the Sea of Galilee south to the Gulf of Aqabah, taking in the Jordan River.

NUMBERS AND DEUTERONOMY

Arad: A city in the area of the Negeb, which was conquered by the Israelites during the conquest of Canaan.

Aram: Another name for Syria.

Argob: A territory assigned by Moses to the tribe of Manasseh; its location is uncertain.

Ark: The portable chest carried inside the tabernacle while the Israelites were wandering in the wilderness. It was thought to contain the presence of God.

Arnon: A river that flowed from the northeast into the Dead Sea.

Aroer: A city in the Amorite kingdom, east of the Jordan River.

Asher: One of the twelve tribes of Israel.

Asherim: Cult objects used in Canaanite worship; they represented fertility goddesses.

Asshur: Another name for Assyria.

Ataroth: A town that Gad and Reuben requested for their possession.

Atharim: A place of uncertain location through which the Israelites moved while under the leadership of Moses; could also mean *spies* or *tracks*.

Atroth-shophan: A city built by the tribe of Gad; it previously belonged to Sihon, king of the Amorites.

Avvim: A people living in Canaan before the Israelites arrived; they were destroyed by the Caphtorim.

Azmon: A city in southern Judah.

Baal-meon: A city in the northern portion of Moab, later inhabited by the tribe of Reuben.

Balaam: A seer who was summoned by Balak, king of Moab, to curse Israel.

Balak: The king of Moab who summoned Balaam to curse the Israelites.

Bamoth: Location where the Israelites stopped on their way to Moab; located somewhere in the Transjordan.

Bamoth-baal: A longer form of the name Bamoth (see above).

Bashan: A territory north and east of the Jordan River.

Bdellium: A precious stone, or perhaps a sticky substance; the term is used to describe manna.

Beeroth: A city located between the territory of Benjamin and Ephraim.

Benejaakan: A place in the territory of Edom where the Israelites encamped.

Beon: Probably another name for Baal-meon.

Beor: The father of Balaam, the seer who was summoned to curse Israel.

Benjamin: One of the tribes of Israel.

Bethharam: A city of Gad, in the Jordan valley.

Bethnimrah: A city of Gad in the Jordan valley.

Bezer: A city of Reuben that was designated as a city of refuge.

Booty: Possessions of an enemy, taken by the victor after a battle.

Bread of the Presence: Twelve loaves of bread, arranged in rows on a special table inside of the tabernacle.

Caleb: One of the men sent by Moses to spy out the land of Canaan; he represented the tribe of Judah.

Canaan: The name of the territory of Palestine, before the Israelites entered it.

Caphtor(im): The territory that was home to the Philistines originally. Its location is uncertain.

Censer: A shallow container that was used to carry live coals from sacrifices.

Chemosh: The name of the Moabite god.

Dan: One of the twelve tribes of Israel.

Dathan: Brother of Abiram; together they led a rebellion against Moses in the wilderness.

Dibon: A city in Moab that later became a possession of the tribe of Gad.

Eber: An ancestor of the Hebrews.

Edom: A territory southeast of Palestine; its inhabitants warred off and on with the Israelites.

Edrei: The city inhabited by Og, the king of Bashan.

Eldad: An Israelite who prophesied inside the limits of the camp.

Eleazar: A son of Aaron; father of Phinehas.

Eliab: An Israelite elder who represented the tribe of Zebulun.

Elizaphan: The leader of the Kohathites in the wilderness.

Emim: Ancient inhabitants of the Transjordan, known for their large size.

Ephah: A dry measure about the size of a tenth of a homer.

Ephraim: One of the sons of Joseph; father of the tribe of Ephraim. Also used as a designation for the people of Israel.

Euphrates River: A river in western Asia; often associated with the Tigris River, which is nearby.

Evi: A Midianite king killed by the Israelite army.

Ezion-geber: A city in the Arabah where the Israelites encamped on their wilderness journey.

Gad: One of the twelve tribes of Israel.

Gaddi: One of the men Moses sent to spy out the land of Canaan.

Gaddiel: One of the men Moses sent to spy out the land of Canaan.

Gaza: One of the five main cities of the Philistines, located along the Mediterranean coast.

Gemalli: One of the men Moses sent to spy out the land of Canaan; he was from the tribe of Dan.

Gerah: One twentieth of a shekel.

Gershon: One of the three sons of Levi.

Geshurites: The people who lived in Geshur, a territory in northeastern Palestine.

Geuel: One of the men Moses sent to spy out the land of Canaan; he was from the tribe of Gad.

Gilead: Could be the name of a territory, a tribe, or a city; located east of the Jordan River.

Gilgal: Name of at least three locations mentioned in the Old Testament. In Numbers and Deuteronomy, Gilgal was located near Jericho.

Girgashites: A Canaanite tribe conquered by the Israelites in the conquest.

Golan: A city of refuge, located in the territory of Bashan.

Hamath: An important city in the region of Syria, north of

Palestine.

Havoth-jair: A group of sixty towns located in the region of Bashan.

Hazar-enan: A city located in between Israel and Hammath.

Hazeroth: A place where the Israelites encamped during their wilderness journey; Miriam and Aaron disputed with Moses here. Its location in the Sinai wilderness is unknown.

Hebron: An important city located directly west of the central portion of the Dead Sea, south of Jerusalem. Also the name of one of the sons of Kohath.

Hepher: One of the clans within the tribe of Manasseh.

Heshbon: An important city in northern Moab.

Hin: A liquid measure equal to approximately one gallon.

Hittites: An ancient people inhabiting a portion of the land of Canaan before the Israelites arrived there.

Hivites: A people inhabiting Canaan before the arrival of the Israelites.

Hoglah: One of Zelophehad's five daughters.

Homer: A dry measure equaling about ten ephahs, or about five bushels.

Horites: An ancient people inhabiting the territory of Seir; perhaps an early name for the Edomites.

Hormah: A city of undetermined location; often used to indicate the southern portion of Israel's territory.

Hoshea: Another name for Joshua.

Hur: One of five Midianite kings slain by the Israelite army under Moses.

Hyssop: A bushy shrub used in purification rites in ancient Israel.

Igal: The spy sent from the tribe of Issachar when Moses sent spies to look at the land of Canaan.

Issachar: One of the twelve tribes of Israel.

Ithamar: One of the sons of Aaron; a priest.

Iye-abarim: An Israelite encampment in southern Moab.

Izhar: One of the sons of Kohath; a Levite.

Jabbok: A tributary of the Jordan River, north of the Dead Sea.

Jahaz: A city in the Transjordan where Sihon, king of the

Amorites, was defeated by the Israelites.

Jair: One of the sons of Manasseh.

Jazer: An Amorite city in the territory of Gilead.

Jebusites: Ancient peoples who inhabited the land of Canaan before the arrival of the Israelites.

Jephunneh: The father of Caleb.

Jericho: Location of an important battle during the conquest of Canaan; northeast of the city of Jerusalem, on the bank of the Jordan River.

Jordan River: The main river of Palestine; it flows north to south from the Sea of Galilee to the Dead Sea.

Joseph: One of the twelve tribes of Israel; sometimes divided into the half-tribes of Ephraim and Manasseh.

Joshua: The son of Nun; leader of the Israelites in their conquest of Canaan; successor to Moses.

Jotbathah: An encampment of the Israelites during their wilderness journey.

Judah: One of the twelve tribes of Israel.

Kadesh: Also called Kadesh-barnea; an oasis located just south of Palestine; the Israelites stopped here first after leaving Mount Sinai.

Kadesh-barnea: See Kadesh.

Kain: Another name for the tribe of the Kenites.

Kedemoth: A levitical city in the territory of Reuben.

Kenites: An ancient people inhabiting the territory of Canaan before the Israelites arrived there.

King's Highway: A road through Canaan that the Israelites traveled under the leadership of Moses.

Kiriathaim: A city of Moab that was later possessed by the tribe of Reuben.

Kiriath-huzoth: A city in Moab to which Balaam was taken by Balak.

Kittim: The Hebrew name for the region of Cyprus.

Kohath: The second son of Levi; the grandfather of Miriam, Moses, and Aaron.

Levites: One of the twelve tribes of Israel; responsible for the functions associated with the tabernacle and worship.

Libni: A family of Levite priests who lived in the vicinity of Hebron.

Machi: One of the tribe of Gad; he was sent by Moses to spy out the land of Canaan.

Mahlah: One of Zelophehad's five daughters.

Manasseh: Sometimes indicates one of the twelve tribes of Israel; brother of Ephraim and son of Joseph.

Manna: A sticky substance provided by God for the Israelites to eat while in the wilderness. Symbolizes the fact that God provides for the people's needs.

Massah: A place of encampment of the Israelites while on their wilderness journey. Always associated with Meribah.

Medad: An Israelite who prophesied inside the camp rather than at the tent of meeting, when the elders were endowed with God's spirit.

Medeba: A city in the Transjordan, near the entrance to the Dead Sea.

Mercy seat: A small structure made of gold and located inside the tabernacle; two cherubim were located on top of it.

Meribah: A station on the Israelites' wilderness journey; located in the Wilderness of Zin.

Michael: The man from the tribe of Asher, sent by Moses to spy out the land of Canaan.

Midian: Its king cooperated with Balak, king of Moab, to bring Balaam to curse the Israelites; the Midianites may have lived in northwest Arabia.

Milcah: One of Zelophehad's five daughters.

Miriam: Sister of Moses and Aaron; daughter of Jochebed.

Moab: A territory in the Transjordan, located east of the Dead Sea.

Moserah: A station of the Israelites while on their wilderness journey.

Nadab: Brother of Abihu, son of Aaron. See *Abihu.*

Nahbi: A man from the tribe of Naphtali; he was sent by Moses to spy out the land of Canaan.

Naphtali: One of the twelve tribes of Israel.

Nazirite: A religious sect that included persons who vowed to abstain from alcohol and from cutting their hair.

Negeb: A desert region to the south of the land of Canaan.

Nobah: An elder from the tribe of Manasseh who figured prominently in the conquest of Canaan.

Nun: The father of Joshua.

Oboth: A site in Moab in which the Israelites encamped during their wilderness journey.

Og: A king of Bashan during the time of the conquest of Canaan.

Palti: A leader in the tribe of Benjamin; Moses sent him to spy out the land of Canaan.

Peleth: A leader of the tribe of Reuben, who participated in Korah's rebellion against Moses.

Perizzites: An ancient people who inhabited Canaan before the arrival of the Israelites.

Pethor: The home of Balaam, who was called by Balak to curse the Israelites.

Phinehas: The son of Eleazar, who was the son of Aaron the priest.

Raphu: The father of Palti; Moses sent him to spy out the land of Canaan.

Reba: One of the five Midianite kings who were destroyed by the Israelites.

Rekem: One of the five Midianite kings who were destroyed by the Israelites.

Reuben: One of the twelve tribes of Israel.

Salecah: A city located in Bashan; later was possessed by the tribe of Gad.

Salt Sea: Another name for the Dead Sea.

Sea of Chinnereth: Another name for the Sea of Galilee.

Seir: A mountain in the northern portion of the territory of Judah.

Sethur: One of the elders of the tribe of Asher; he was sent by Moses to spy out the land of Canaan.

Shammua: One of the elders of the tribe of Reuben; he was sent by Moses to spy out the land of Canaan.

Shaphat: One of the elders of the tribe of Simeon; he was sent by Moses to spy out the land of Canaan.

Shekel: In earliest times it was a weight; later on the name was used to designate a coin.

Sheol: The underworld; where the dead lived as shades.

Sheshai: A son of Anak, who was living in Canaan at the time the Israelites arrived there.

Shimei: The son of Gershom; a grandson of Levi.

Shittim: A location northeast of the Dead Sea, in the territory of Moab, where the Israelites encamped during their wilderness journey.

Sibmah: A city inherited by the Reubenites after the defeat of the Amorite king, Sihon.

Sihon: The king of the Amorites who was defeated by the Israelites as they passed through his territory.

Simeon: One of the twelve tribes of Israel.

Sinai: The mountain on which Moses received the Ten Commandments, and from which the Israelites journeyed afterwards.

Sirion: Another name for Mount Hermon.

Sodi: An elder of the tribe of Zebulun; Moses sent him to spy out the land of Canaan.

Sojourner: A foreigner living temporarily in another territory, and who is subject to the laws of that community.

Spoil: Booty taken after an army has defeated a town or city.

Susi: An elder from the tribe of Manasseh, who was sent by Moses to spy out the land of Canaan.

Taberah: A site of unknown location where the Israelites encamped while on their wilderness journey.

Tabernacle: A portable tent that was carried through the wilderness by the Israelites; God was thought to dwell inside.

Talmai: A son of Anak, who lived in Hebron before the Israelites arrived there.

Tent of meeting: Another name for the tabernacle.

Thummim: With Urim, items by which persons consulted God about particular questions. Perhaps these were small metal objects.

Tirzah: One of Zelophehad's five daughters.

Tithe: One-tenth of one's property, donated to support the priesthood.

Unleavened bread: Bread baked without yeast and used in Israel's religious ritual.

Urim: See *Thummim.*

Uzziel: One of the sons of Kohath; the grandson of Levi.

Valley of Zered: The land surrounding the stream the Israelites crossed at the end of their wilderness wanderings.

Vophsi: An elder in the tribe of Naphtali; Moses sent him to spy out the land of Canaan.

Zebulun: One of the twelve tribes of Israel.

Zelophehad: An elder from the tribe of Manasseh, whose daughters demanded his inheritance at the time of his death.

Zin: A wilderness north of Paran, through which the Israelites traveled on their wilderness journey.

Zippor: The father of Balak, the king of Moab who summoned Balak to curse the Israelites.

Guide to Pronunciation

Abihu: Ah-BEE-hoo
Abiram: Ah-BEE-ram
Akrabbim: Ah-krah-BEEM
Amalekites: Ah-MAA-leh-kites
Ammonites: AH-moh-nites
Amorites: AH-moh-rites
Amram: Ahm-RAHM
Anakim: Ah-nah-KEEM
Arabah: ARE-uh-bah
Arad: ARE-ad
Argob: Ar-GOBE
Arnon: ARE-non
Aroer: Ah-ROH-er
Asherim: Ash-eh-REEM
Ataroth: Ah-tah-ROTHE
Atharim: Ah-thah-REEM
Avvim: Ah-VEEM
Azmon: AZ-mon
Baal-meon: Bah-ALL-may-OWN
Bamoth: Bah-MOTHE
Bashan: Bah-SHAHN
Beeroth: Buh-ay-ROTHE
Beon: Beh-OWN
Beor: Beh-ORE
Bethharam: Beth-hah-RAHM
Bezer: BEH-zer
Caphtorim: Caf-toh-REEM
Chemosh: CHEH-mosh

NUMBERS AND DEUTERONOMY

Dibon: Dih-BONE
Edom: EE-dum
Eleazar: Eh-lee-AY-zar
Eliab: EH-lee-ab
Elizaphan: Eh-lee-ZAH-fahn
Emim: Eh-MEEM
Ephah: EE-fah
Ephraim: EE-frah-eem
Ezion-geber: EH-zee-own-GEH-ber
Gerah: Geh-RAH
Hamath: Hah-MAHTH
Hazeroth: Hah-zeh-ROTHE
Heshbon: HESH-bon
Issachar: IH-zuh-car
Iye-abarim: EYE-ah-bah-REEM
Jair: Jah-EER
Jephunneh: Jeh-FOO-neh
Jotbathah: JOT-bah-thah
Kadesh: KAH-desh
Kedemoth: Keh-deh-MOTHE
Kiriathaim: Kir-ee-ah-THAH-yim
Kohath: KOH-hath
Manasseh: Muh-NASS-eh
Medeba: Meh-deh-BAH
Meribah: Mare-ih-BAH
Naphtali: Naff-TAL-lee
Oboth: Oh-BOTHE
Perizzites: PEH-rih-zites
Phinehas: Fih-NAY-hass
Salecah: Sah-leh-KAH
Sihon: SEE-hun
Sirion: SEER-ee-on
Taberah: Tah-beh-RAH
Thummim: THOO-mim
Urim: YOOR-im
Uziel: Oo-zee-ELL
Zelophehad: Zeh-LOH-feh-had

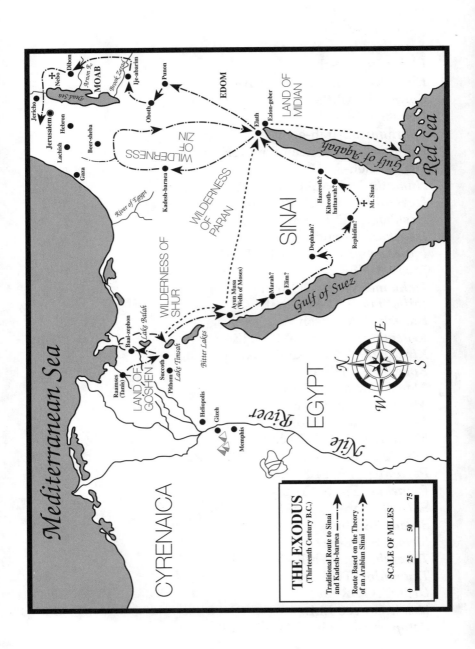

THE EXODUS
(Thirteenth Century B.C.)

Traditional Route to Sinai
and Kadesh-barnea ——▶

Route Based on the Theory
of an Arabian Sinai ----▶

SCALE OF MILES

0   25   50   75

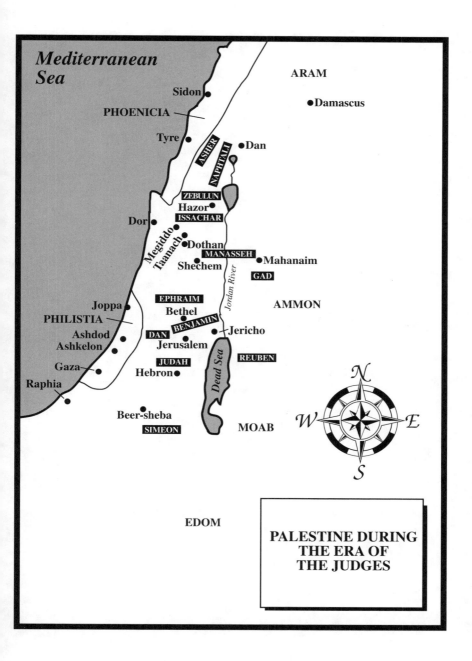

Mediterranean Sea

ARAM

Sidon

PHOENICIA

•Damascus

Tyre

ASHER

•Dan

NAPHTALI

ZEBULUN

Hazor

Dor

ISSACHAR

Megiddo
Taanach

•Dothan

MANASSEH

Shechem

•Mahanaim

Jordan River

GAD

Joppa

EPHRAIM

PHILISTIA

Bethel

AMMON

Ashdod
Ashkelon

DAN

BENJAMIN

•Jericho

Jerusalem

Gaza

JUDAH

Dead Sea

REUBEN

Raphia

Hebron•

Beer-sheba

SIMEON

MOAB

EDOM

**PALESTINE DURING
THE ERA OF
THE JUDGES**